T0361251

FINANCIAL VOLATILITY AND REAL ECONOMIC ACTIVITY

*I dedicate this book to
Anne, Ciara, Nicholas, Patrick
and my dear mother,
Elizabeth.*

Financial Volatility and Real Economic Activity

KEVIN JAMES DALY
University of Western Sydney (Macarthur)

Routledge
Taylor & Francis Group
LONDON AND NEW YORK

First published 1999 by Ashgate Publishing

Reissued 2018 by Routledge
2 Park Square, Milton Park, Abingdon, Oxon, OX14 4RN
711 Third Avenue, New York, NY 10017, USA

Routledge is an imprint of the Taylor & Francis Group, an informa business

Publisher's Note
The publisher has gone to great lengths to ensure the quality of this reprint but points out that some imperfections in the original copies may be apparent.

Disclaimer
The publisher has made every effort to trace copyright holders and welcomes correspondence from those they have been unable to contact.

A Library of Congress record exists under LC control number: 98073755

ISBN 13: 978-1-138-31507-5 (hbk)
ISBN 13: 978-0-429-45657-2 (ebk)

Contents

List of Figures

List of Tables

Acknowledgements

This book represents the culmination of some five years of work over which time I have been preoccupied with understanding the intricate relationships between Financial Market Volatility and Real Economic Activity. I am indebted to my Ph.D. thesis supervisor, Professor Colm Kearney, whose thoughtfulness and critical and analytical suggestions over the years have made my Ph.D. studies an enjoyable and thoroughly rewarding experience. In particular I wish to thank Colm for his co-authorship of Chapter Four, which provides a detailed empirical analysis investigating the 'Causes of Stock Market Volatility in Australia'.

I also wish to thank Professor Anis Chowdhury who has been influential and inspiring in his comments on numerous drafts of this research project. His detailed and creative advice generated many critical refinements. Professor Satya Paul was also very helpful with the final stages of putting the thesis together.

Finally, I would like to express my gratitude to Mrs Christine Davis and the entire staff at Ashgate Publishing for their kind and skilful assistance and to Ms Lizette DeLacey from the University of Western Sydney for her efficiency and help with compiling the final copy of this book.

Abstract

The issue of financial volatility, especially since financial deregulation, has given rise to concerns regarding the effects of increased financial volatility on real economic activity. Two issues represent a substantial challenge to financial economists with respect to these concerns. The first relates to the identification of the causes of increased volatility in financial markets. Identification is a first step toward increasing both financial economists' and policy makers' understanding of the interrelated causes of financial volatility. The second requires linking the effects of increased financial volatility to the real sector of the economy; this involves examining the channels through which financial volatility influences fundamental economic variables.

In order to address these two issues, the analysis initially develops and estimates a model which is capable of explaining the financial and business cycle determinants of movements in the conditional volatility of the Australian All Industrials stock market index. Evidence suggests that a significant linkage exists between the conditional volatility of the stock market and the conditional volatility of the money supply. Models are then developed to examine how monetary volatility is transmitted to the volatility of financial asset prices, inflation and real output in an open economy. A Markowitz efficient portfolio is constructed to eliminate diversifiable financial risk and the model is estimated for Australian data. Incorporation of a second model which allows a level of diversifiable financial risk to remain allows comparisons to be made. The results suggest that the transmission of monetary volatility impulses to real output occurs predominantly *via* the share market.

Further empirical analysis reveals that the financing of fiscal policy actions have significant effects on exchange rate volatility across major economies. In the light of this evidence, fiscal policy appears to have an undesired volatility-magnifying effect even though the initial object of policy may have been the desire to raise the level and dampen the volatility of nominal output. Formal tests analysing the effect of exchange rate volatility on trade flows vindicates recent theoretical models which suggest that volatility associated with floating exchange rates does not impede trade flows. Overall the results indicate that while financial volatility has increased to some extent over the last decade or so, this volatility has been transferred non-uniformly towards increasing volatility of both real and financial activity.

1 Introduction

Overview

It is commonly acknowledged that the process of extensive financial deregulation which has occurred in Australia over the past decade and a half has resulted in a rise in financial volatility. Examples which readily spring to mind include the exchange rate, interest rates and perhaps the stock market also. These developments have induced economists to find answers to the following interrelated issues:

- Has increased exchange rate volatility in the post-float era impeded trade flows?
- What can be said about the validity of structural models of exchange rates?
- What are the causes of financial asset volatility?
- Does increased volatility in the financial sector affect the real sector?
- What effect do Government policies via fiscal and monetary instruments have on financial asset price volatility?

This book contributes to the literature on these issues by conducting an empirical investigation of the effects of financial volatility on real economic activity.

To begin the investigation, the book focuses on the "causes of stock market volatility." An important issue here is to examine the extent to which volatility in the stock market is a reflection of fundamental macroeconomic volatility. The issue of stock market volatility has received much attention in the finance literature. Amongst the main questions which have been addressed include what are the important causes of stock market volatility, has it increased over time, has international financial integration lead to faster transmission of volatility across international stock markets, and what role, if any, ought regulators play in the process? This book contributes to the literature on the causes of stock market volatility by examining the determinants of movements in the volatility of equity returns in a small, internationally integrated stock market. The Australian stock market serves as an especially illuminating example in this regard insofar as it is increasingly integrated with the important international stock markets throughout Asia and the world.

1

An interrelated though complex area investigated in this book concerns the impact of monetary and fiscal policy initiatives on the volatility of financial asset prices and other macroeconomic variables. While it is acknowledged that Government stabilization policies via fiscal and monetary policy instruments are ultimately targeted at raising the level and reducing the volatility of nominal output, the conduct of such a strategy may have indirect effects which cause the volatility of financial asset prices to increase. In this regard the impact of Government fiscal financing innovations on exchange rates is examined. With respect to monetary influences, the book examines how monetary volatility is transmitted to the volatility of financial asset prices, inflation and real output in an open economy. Despite a voluminous literature on the appropriate design and implementation of fiscal and monetary policies in economies which are open to international trade in commodities, services and financial assets, the issue remains controversial.

Continuing the theme of analysing the relationship between price volatility and real economic activity, the book examines the impact of the post-float increase in exchange rate volatility on trade flows within a multi-country dataset. Despite the predictions of the early proponents of flexible exchange rates, the actual experience with floating rates since the demise of the Bretton Woods system in the early 1970s has been characterised by large fluctuations in both nominal and real exchange rates. Many economists have expressed concern that this rise in exchange rate volatility has reduced the allocational efficiency of the international monetary system. An important ingredient of this concern has been the extent to which the volume of international trade flows has been impeded.

Structure of Book

Given the emphasis on volatility in this book as well as its widespread use in financial economics, it is important to first develop a clear understanding of the term. In chapter two volatility is defined, the sources of volatility are examined, techniques employed for its measurement are evaluated, examples of their application are given and conceptual issues and conflicts involved in measuring volatility are discussed.

Chapter three provides a framework for the research questions investigated in the book by reviewing the related theoretical and empirical literature. The chapter presents a historical overview of the literature, emphasising the links between financial volatility and macroeconomic activity. The motivation for examining these links is discussed. Theoretical models used to value financial assets are scrutinised and compared to empirical evidence. The role of volatility within the context of the efficient market hypothesis is analysed, in particular the relationship between market fundamentals and financial asset pricing models is explored by comprehensively reviewing the literature on this subject. The relationships between financial instability and macroeconomic activity are investigated from both developed and developing countries' perspective. Monetary volatility and its relationship with both real and nominal activity is discussed. The monetary transmission mechanism is evaluated, the theoretical debate over exogenous versus endogenous money is discussed and the empirical evidence on monetary policy performance within the Australian context is reviewed. Finally, the role of fiscal and monetary policy and their effects on both real and financial volatility are mentioned.

Chapter four develops and estimates an empirical model which is capable of explaining the financial and business cycle determinants of movements in the conditional volatility of the Australian All Industrials stock market index. The model employs a low frequency monthly dataset for Australia including stock market returns, interest rates, inflation, the money supply, industrial production and the current account deficit over the period from July 1972 to January 1994. The analysis presented is interpretable as an extension of the low frequency analysis of Schwert (1989) who did not include international factors such as the current account deficit and the exchange rate in his investigation of the causes of stock market volatility in the US. Previous research on the volatility of the Australian stock market includes the work of Brailsford and Faff (1993) and Kearns and Pagan (1993), both of whom examined the relative explanatory power of alternative models of conditional volatility, but neither of whom related stock market volatility to the volatility of financial and business cycle variables.

Chapter five examines how monetary volatility is transmitted to the volatility of financial asset prices, inflation and real output. The chapter formulates and estimates empirical models which are capable of explaining the financial and business cycle determinants of movement in the conditional volatility of the Australian All Industrials stock market index. The estimated models employ a monthly dataset which includes the money supply, the interest rate, the share market, the foreign exchange rate, inflation and real output over the period from January 1972 to January 1994.

Chapter six examines the extent to which innovations in the stance of Government's fiscal policy and in its method of financing impact on the foreign exchange value of a country's currency. In view of the considerable uncertainty which pervades appropriate specification of the relevant theoretical models, the empirical analysis of this chapter adopts the vector autoregressive approach which constitutes an unrestricted reduced form of some unknown structural model. Using quarterly data models are estimated for seven countries (Australia, Britain, Canada, France, Germany, Italy and the US) over the period of floating exchange rates from 1975(2) to 1995(2).

The purpose of Chapter seven is to examine the extent to which exchange rate volatility impedes bilateral trade flows since the introduction of floating exchange rates after the demise of the Bretton Woods system in the early 1970s. Employing an eight country dataset which spans the period 1978(1)-1992(2), the chapter estimates empirical models of bilateral trade flows in which the null hypothesis of zero exchange rate volatility effect is tested against the alternative hypothesis of non-zero volatility effect.

Finally, Chapter eight provides a synopsis and discussion of the results of the study and points to the avenues for further research.

The Background to the Research Question

From a Keynesian perspective, volatility may arise as a result of the increased pace of financial transactions which financial liberalisation allows. Keynes, (1964) and Singh (1993) argue that where volatility forces investors to reduce their time horizons for both profit-seeking and loss-minimising reasons, there is a paradoxical effect of inducing increased volatility. This implies that increases in financial market volatility with frequent and severe price swings might be much more apt to induce short-term speculative investment practices, which may lead to reductions in real-sector investment activity. Grabel (1995a) makes the point that the liquidity of modern financial markets brings about an independence of financial asset values from underlying 'fundamentals' which imparts an extreme variability to these values. Modern financial instruments afford the apparent protection of instantaneous withdrawal of funds by transforming illiquid real sector investments in plant and equipment into financial claims that can change hands as quickly as the technological structures permit. The ability to flee all such instruments for money provides a degree of apparent security to the financial investor that is not available to the industrial corporation that has undertaken long-term capital investment. Other scholars including Singh (1993), Calamanti (1983) and Samuels and Yacout (1981) argue that the expansion of stock markets in developing countries increased speculative activity relative to total economic activity with the consequence increased financial crises and a misallocation of savings and investment to the detriment of real sector growth and stability.

Whether and to what degree financial market volatility is an impediment to real sector growth and stability depends on the links between financial volatility and real sector activity. Yet empirical research to date has failed to explore satisfactorily either the links between financial market volatility and real economic activity or the techniques appropriate for measuring price volatility.

The fundamental question examined in this book concerns the relationship between the volatility of financial asset prices and macroeconomic activity. Although the direction of causation (i.e. whether primarily from financial to real activity or *vice versa*) is not always important to the subject matter of the book, the empirical analysis investigating the issues leans heavily on the causal direction running from financial volatility to real economic activity. The book shows that volatile financial asset prices have been transferred towards increasing volatility of both real and financial activity.

4

Recent literature indicates a revival of interest in the relationship between the financial sector and macroeconomic activity. Gertler (1988) states, 'Recently, interest has grown in exploring the possible links between the financial system and aggregate economic behavior'. The results of Chen et al (1986), imply that stock prices are driven by innovations in economic variables. Kim and Wu (1987) incorporate a multifactor return-generating process in the traditional Capital Asset Pricing Model (CAPM) and find that their model is capable of directly utilising macroeconomic variables in defining factors. Chang and Pinegar (1989, 1990) examine different economic variables to study their interrelationships with the stock market. They use bivariate Granger tests of causality which indicated that the returns on large firms' stocks predict seasonal real growth at least six months in advance. Darrat (1988,1990) investigates the relationship between aggregate stock returns and a number of macroeconomic variables, including monetary and fiscal policy. He also uses multivariate, Granger-causality modeling techniques to test whether changes in Canadian stock returns are caused by economic variables (base money and fiscal deficits). His results show lagged changes in fiscal deficits Granger-cause returns. Friedman and Laibson (1993) examine the economic implications of extraordinary movements in stock prices. Dhakal, Kandil and Sharma (1993) provide evidence of a causal impact of volatility in share prices on fluctuations in real output. Tarhan (1993) attempts to provide an economic explanation of volatility by examining the connection between volatility and policy, and suggests that policy responds to volatility in the exchange rates and also to volatility in the short-term interest rates. Galeotti and Schiantarelli (1994) show that changes in fundamentals have a greater impact on investment decisions than changes in non-fundamentals.

Methods and Motives

The research topic of this book examines the effects of financial volatility on economic activity. The motivation behind this study is the fact that the profession of finance and economics knows little about the causes of volatility and the links between financial volatility and real economic activity. One important reason for this gap in our knowledge is due to the lack of a theory which explains how volatility behaves. Such a theory is unlikely to develop, however, until the true price setting process in financial markets is known. But this may never happen. Meanwhile, empirical examination of volatility from various sources appears to be the most productive avenue of current research.

Throughout this book, various statistical and econometric methods have been applied in an attempt to increase our understanding of volatility, ranging from Autoregressive Conditional Heteroscedastic (ARCH) models to the Vector Autoregression (VAR) approach. Chapter two discusses the various techniques that have been employed to measure volatility, while Chapter three provides an overview of the existing empirical evidence on the relationship between financial volatility and real economic activity.

Chapter four examines the causes of Stock Market Volatility in Australia. A novel feature of this analysis is the estimation strategy employed to overcome problems which pervade some recent related research in the finance literature. Specifically, the procedure of Davidian and Caroll (1987) which has been used by Schwert (1989) and others to model conditional volatility is problematic. Schwert's (1989) vector autoregressive model of the determination of conditional stock market volatility, along with other research which employs the same methodology, suffer from the generated regressors problem which yields inefficient estimates, introduces bias into a number of diagnostic test statistics and generates potentially invalid inferences. This problem is overcome in chapters four and five by jointly estimating the equation for the conditional volatility of stock market returns, together with the equations determining the conditional volatilities of all variables included in the model using the Generalised Least Squares (GLS) estimation procedure together with the Hendry general-to-specific modelling strategy.

Chapter five of this book empirically models how monetary volatility is transmitted to the volatility of financial asset prices, inflation and real output, for the Australian economy. A Markowitz efficient portfolio is constructed to eliminate diversifiable financial risk, and estimation by Generalised Least Squares on monthly Australian data using the general-to-specific estimation strategy overcomes the generated regressors problem in related ARCH-type models. In particular, monetary growth volatility is transmitted to output volatility *via* the volatility of financial asset prices in two versions of the model. In the first version, a Markowitz efficient portfolio of financial assets is constructed to eliminate diversifiable risk between financial assets. This portfolio therefore contains only nondiversifiable risk or systemic financial risk. The implication of this portfolio structure for modelling the transmission of monetary volatility to the rest of the economy is that since the remaining financial risk cannot be diversified away, this should be the focus of the transmission mechanism in a modern financial system. By way of comparison, a second version of the model is presented which retains each of the financial assets with unitary weights so that a level of diversifiable financial risk remains.

In Chapter six it is argued that the theoretical open economy macroeconomic models of recent vintage yield divergent predictions about how variations in the stance of fiscal policy and in the method of its financing impinge upon the exchange rate. In view of the considerable uncertainty which pervades appropriate specification of these macromodels, the empirical analysis adopts the VAR approach which constitutes an unrestricted reduced form of some unknown structural model. The analysis constructs a five equation VAR model which has Government Expenditure, Tax Receipts, Money (M1), the Current Account and the Foreign Exchange Rate as dependent variables.

6

Finally, Chapter seven investigates the extent to which exchange rate volatility impedes bilateral trade flows. In addition to exchange rate volatility, other factors that have been posited to affect trade flows include real economic activity, costs and prices which feature in the theoretical framework. The empirical analysis differs from the majority of previous research by appropriately specifying the models in terms of the order of integration of the data and the equation dynamics.

Contributions and Major Findings

In Chapter two of this book, various techniques used to measure volatility are examined ranging from time invariant measures to time variant measures. It is shown that a weakness of the former measures arises from the underlying assumption that volatility is considered to be constant over time. This observation has led researchers to develop time variant measures based on the assumption that volatility changes over time. The introduction of the original ARCH model by Engle (1982) has spawned an ever increasing variety of models such as GARCH, EGARCH, NARCH, ARCH-M MARCH and the Taylor-Schwert model. It was noted that the degree of sophistication in developing these models has increased. This, no doubt, is to allow the models to capture various characteristics of economic and financial time series data including volatility clustering, leverage effects and the persistence of volatility itself. A feature of these more elaborate models is that while they generally obtain a better fit to the data in-sample they tend to go off track when taken out-of-sample. The objective of any technique which purports to measure volatility is to provide a method of capturing the movement or change in a variable over past and/or future time periods, a key concern here is the lack of a direct theory which predicts how volatility will behave.

Chapter three provides a review of the literature which examines the link between financial volatility and the real economic activity. In the chapter the material examined is classified into three broad areas. First, the literature on the major determinants of stock market volatility is examined. This review points to a number of determinants which can be classified into fundamental and non-fundamental causes. The chapter makes the point that while we know that stock market volatility changes over time, that it tends to cluster, that it is persistent, and that volatility peaks are associated with price declines, we still know little about the fundamental causes of volatility in financial markets. The chapter also examines a theory of financial instability (proposed by Minsky, 1977) and its links to macroeconomic activity. The point made here is that whilst this theory best describes events leading up to what is appropriately termed financial crises, the theory does not explain the causes of increased financial volatility over recent times or the concomitant effects on real economic activity. Finally this chapter investigates the issue of monetary volatility and its effects on financial and non-financial activity. The chapter examines the role of money in business cycle

7

fluctuations and contends that the role of money remains a controversial issue without a unifying theory. The chapter then reviews the empirical evidence on monetary policy as conducted in Australia over the past twenty years.

While chapters two and three contain survey material, the novel contributions of this book reside in chapters four through seven. Specifically, Chapter four investigates the causes of stock market volatility by examining the determinants of movements in the volatility of equity returns in the Australian stock market. The most significant determinants of stock market volatility are found to be the volatility of inflation and interest rates which are directly associated with stock market volatility, while the volatility of industrial production, the current account deficit and the money supply are indirectly associated with stock market volatility. Amongst these variables, the most significant determinant of conditional volatility in the Australian stock market is the degree of volatility which exists in the money supply. By contrast, no evidence is found of a statistically significant relationship between foreign exchange market volatility and stock market volatility in Australia.

Chapter five contributes to the literature on the extent to which monetary growth volatility is transmitted to the real sector of the macroeconomy. The analysis contains some novel features. Unlike most previous related research which focuses on the transmission mechanisms from monetary volatility to the *levels* of financial asset prices and macroeconomic variables, the analysis in Chapter five focuses on the transmission mechanisms from monetary growth volatility to the volatility of financial asset prices and the volatility of macroeconomic variables. The transmission mechanism employs a Markowitz efficient portfolio comprising bonds, stocks and foreign exchange which eliminates the diversifiable risk associated with holding these assets. This portfolio therefore contains only the systemic financial risk which cannot be diversified away by sophisticated market participants, and it is intuitive that this should be the transmission mechanism that is examined in a modern financial system. The major findings are that the transmission of monetary volatility impulses to real output occurs predominantly through the share market rather than through interest rates, with no significant effect operating through the foreign exchange market. This is of considerable interest insofar as it tends to vindicate the view that the volatility associated with floating exchange rates does not seem to spill over to real output. This evidence also corroborates the finding by Dhakal et al (1993) that changes in money supply indirectly bring about a causal impact on the volatility of share prices which impacts on the rate of growth of real output.

Chapter six attempts an empirical exploration of the effects of fiscal policy and its method of financing upon the exchange rate of seven major economies. In view of the considerable uncertainty which pervades appropriate specification of the relevant theoretical models, the empirical methodology adopted is that of an unrestricted vector autoregressive approach (VAR) with orthogonalising conditions given by the recursive ordering according to the method proposed by Sims (1980). The overall results for the seven countries over the recent float show that, in line with the theoretical literature, no clear pattern emerges, with the sign of the effect and the impulse response functions to the shocks varying between countries. The conclusion reached is that no consistent pattern can be found in the exchange rate response to fiscal financing decisions across seven major advanced industrial economies.

The purpose of Chapter seven is to examine the extent to which exchange rate volatility impedes bilateral trade flows. The major finding is that exchange rate volatility is at least as likely to raise trade flows as it is to impede them. Of the 14 bilateral trade flow cases, real exchange rate volatility is significantly and positively related to trade flows in six cases. This empirical result is in line with recent theoretical literature which provides a theoretical basis for a positive effect of exchange rate variability on trade flows. As with previous empirical research on the relationship between exchange rate volatility and trade flows, it is difficult to draw unambiguous policy conclusions. Perhaps the most significant aspect of this work is the importance of comparing the effects of exchange-rate costs of alternative policy options which might be enacted in order to reduce it.

2 Volatility: Issues and Measuring Techniques

Introduction

Volatility is a fundamentally important concept to this thesis. Several reasons have been advanced as to why volatility is an important issue in itself. *Firstly*, when asset prices fluctuate sharply over time differentials as short as one day or less, investors may find it difficult to accept that the explanation for these changes lies in information about fundamental economic factors. This may lead to an erosion of confidence in capital markets and a reduced flow of capital into equity markets. *Secondly*, for individual firms the volatility of the firm is an important factor in determining the probability of bankruptcy. The higher the volatility for a given capital structure, the higher the probability of default. *Thirdly*, volatility is an important factor in determining the bid-ask spread. The higher the volatility of the stock, the wider is the spread between the bid and ask prices of the market maker. The volatility of the stock thus affects the market's liquidity. *Fourthly*, hedging techniques such as portfolio insurance are affected by the volatility level, with the prices of insurance increasing with volatility. *Fifthly*, economic and financial theory suggests that consumers are risk averse. Increased risk associated with a given economic activity should, therefore, see a reduced level of participation in that activity, which will have adverse consequences for investment. *Finally*, increased volatility over time may induce regulatory agencies and providers of capital to force firms to allocate a larger percentage of available capital to cash equivalent investments, to the potential detriment of allocational efficiency. In light of the above, it appears justifiable to discuss volatility in some depth.

The objective of this chapter is to provide an overview of volatility. To date, there exist several reviews on specific models or issues regarding volatility, such as those of Bollerslev, Chou and Kroner (1992), Kupiec (1993) and Bera and Higgins (1993) but there appears to be no coverage of this controversial topic from a broader perspective, providing an insight on volatility to a more general audience of financial economists.

This chapter, begins by providing a background discussion on the question of what is Volatility? followed by an examination of the factors that influence volatility. The next section 'Determinants of Volatility Changes' provides an overview of the models used to measure volatility, and points to some of their inherent weaknesses. The final section summarizes the chapter and draws together the conclusions.

What is Volatility?

Volatility can be described broadly as anything that is changeable or variable. Volatility can be defined as the changeableness of the variable under consideration; the more the variable fluctuates over a period of time, the more volatile the variable is said to be. Volatility is associated with unpredictability, uncertainty and risk. To the general public, the term is synonymous with risk, hence high volatility is thought of as a symptom of market disruption whereby securities are not being priced fairly and the capital market is not functioning as well as it should. Volatility is of enormous importance to everyone involved in the financial markets, where it is thought of more in terms of unpredictability. In this context, volatility is often used to describe dispersion from an expected value, price or model. The deviation of prices from theoretical asset pricing model values, and the variability of traded prices from their sample mean are two examples. As discussed earlier, substantial changes in the volatility of financial market returns are capable of having significant negative effects on risk averse investors. In addition, such changes can also impact on consumption patterns, corporate capital investment decisions, leverage decisions and other business cycle and macroeconomic variables. Traditionally, volatility is viewed as synonymous with variance risk. The trade-off between risk and expected return is the foundation upon which much of modern finance theory such as Capital Asset Pricing Models, Arbitrage Pricing Models and portfolio theory is based. Modern option pricing theory, beginning with Black and Scholes (1973), places volatility in a central role in determining the fair value of an option. In the Black-Scholes option pricing formula, returns volatility of the underlying asset is an important parameter, and its importance is magnified by the fact that it is the only one variable that is not directly observable. Although realised volatility can be computed from historical data, an option's theoretical value depends on the volatility that will be experienced in the future over its entire lifetime. Despite recent scrutiny, relatively little is yet known about the causes of volatility in various financial and commodity markets.

Schwert (1990) shows that an increase in stock market volatility (as measured by percentage change in prices or rates of return)[1] brings an increased chance of large stock price changes of either sign. Most of the markets' highest returns, for example, occurred during the Great Depression from 1929 to 1939. The most commonly used measure of stock return volatility is the standard deviation. Taking a plot of the volatility of monthly returns (measured by the standard deviation) of the listed stocks on the New York Stock Exchange shows the highest periods of volatility this century were recorded from 1929 to 1939 and for October 1987. Shiller (1989) concluded that stock market volatility is excessively high relative to fundamental values. This issue will be explored further in Chapter three. Shiller's work is supported by Spiro (1990), while Schwert (1991) was strongly critical, claiming Shiller's status has little to do with the scientific merits of his work. In terms of percentage stock price movements, over the past few years volatility has increased dramatically for short intervals, with periods of high volatility such as 1987 for equities, 1992 for foreign exchange and 1994 for bonds. Kupiec (1991) shows that over this period stock return volatility increased in many OECD countries. He argues that this higher average volatility recorded in the 1980s was caused by short periods of abnormally high return volatility which raised measures of average volatility for the decade.

What Influences Volatility?

One way of examining the influences on volatility is to calculate volatility over several different frequencies. Historical data shows that some volatility clusters are short-lived, lasting only a few hours, while others last a decade. The primary source of changes in market prices is the arrival of news about an asset's fundamental value. If the news arrives in rapid succession, and if the data is of sufficiently high frequency to pick up the arrival of news, then returns will exhibit a volatility cluster. At higher frequencies, the most likely sources of volatility are the pressures and turbulence induced through trading, often called noise. At lower frequencies, macroeconomic and institutional changes are the most likely influences. The high volatility of the 1930s, for example, is attributed to macroeconomic events. In general, the frequency of data dictates which types of volatility clusters can be seen and therefore measured. Low frequency data allows only low frequency or macroeconomic fluctuations to be seen, while higher frequency data reveals more about the volatility properties.

Determinants of Volatility Changes

Nelson (1996) lists several factors associated with market volatility changes. The more important of these are: (1) *positive serial correlation* in volatility. This means that 'large changes tend to be followed by large changes of either sign and small changes tend to be followed by small changes' (see Mandelbrot, 1963); (2) Fama (1965) and French and Roll (1986) show that *trading and nontrading days* contribute to market volatility. In particular, stock market volatility tends to be higher on Mondays than on other days of the week, reflecting movements of stock prices on a Monday based on information arriving over a 72 hour period, while on other trading days, price movements reflect information arriving over a 24-hour period; (3) *Leverage effects* provide a partial explanation for market volatility changes. When firms' stock prices fall, they become more leveraged and the volatility of its return typically rises. Black (1976) argued, however, that the measured effect of stock price changes on volatility are too large to be explained solely by leverage changes; (4) During *recessions and financial crises* stock market volatility tends to be high. For instance, stock market volatility hit a historic high during the 1930s Great Depression (see Schwert, 1988 and Officer, 1973); and (5) *High nominal interest rates* have been shown to be associated with high market volatility (see Fama and Schwert, 1977; Christie, 1982 and Glosten et al. 1989).

Long-term and Short-term Factors Influencing Volatility

Bearing in mind the above discussion, it appears intuitive to separate the factors that influence volatility into long-term and short-term factors. Amongst the long-term influences on volatility is that of corporate leverage (i.e. debt/ equity ratios). Christie (1982) and Black (1976) identified volatility peaks with stock market price declines, their explanation for this being based on the effects that corporate leverage has on volatility. The argument is essentially circular, because stock price declines will increase financial risk, since the debt/equity ratio has increased. This increase in financial risk will, in turn, increase the expected return to equity which decreases the current stock prices. Schwert (1989) presents evidence of a positive correlation between corporate leverage and volatility. Similar results have been obtained by Black (1976), Christie (1982) and French, Schwert and Stambaugh (1987). Amongst them, French, Schwert and Stambaugh (1987), Officer (1973) and Schwert (1989) have identified an association between volatility peaks and recessions. Major volatility peaks have been associated with the 1930s Great Depression, the OPEC oil crisis of 1974, and the stock market crash of October 1987. Schwert (1989) also showed that the volatility of industrial production is highest during financial recessions.

Factors which influence volatility over the short-term include trading volume, contrarian trade,[2] and the introduction of futures and options.[3] Perhaps the most commented upon of these factors is the association between trading volume and volatility. Market folklore suggests that trading volume is positively associated with volatility. Karpoff (1987) reviewed the theory and evidence on this relationship and concluded that there is strong support for a positive relationship. French and Roll (1986) found that the volatility on the NYSE during trading hours is far greater than during weekend non-trading hours and this is due to the arrival of private rather than public information. By definition, private information can only affect prices through trading, whereas public information can affect prices at any time.

Statistical Measures

A common measure of stock market volatility is the standard deviation of returns. Estimates of sample standard deviation from daily returns serve as a useful measure for characterising the evolution of volatility. This statistic measures the dispersion of returns.

$$\sigma = \sqrt{\sum_{1}^{T} (R - \bar{R})^2 / (T-1)} \qquad (2.0)$$

The standard deviation σ of returns R_t from a sample of T observations is the square root of the average deviation of returns from the average return in the sample, where $\bar{R}$ is the sample average return, $\bar{R} = \Sigma R_t / T$. The standard deviation is a simple but useful measure of volatility because it summarises the probability of seeing extreme values of return. When the sample standard deviation is large, the chance of a large positive or negative return is large. Several studies have used a modification of the standard deviation to estimate volatility. Hooper and Kohlhagen (1978), Cushman (1983), Aschheim *et al* (1993) and Daly (1997a) all use a four quarter moving standard deviation of exchange rates as a proxy for exchange rate volatility.

A measure of volatility which focuses on the uncertainty aspect of volatility is the Root Mean Square Percentage Error (RMSPE). This is a simple and well known measure of prediction errors, and can be represented as follows:

$$RMSPE = 100 \sqrt{\frac{1}{T} \sum_{t=1}^{T} \left(\frac{E_t - \hat{E}_t}{E_t} \right)^2} \qquad (2.1)$$

where E_t represent the actual variable in period t, and $\hat{E}_t$ is the predicted value of the variable. How do we generate $\hat{E}_t$? One approach is to rely on time series techniques such as mechanistic rules (e.g. no-trend, no-change) to more sophisticated processes (e.g. Schwert's (1989) measure) discussed below. A simple method to generate the forecast value $\hat{E}_t$ for period t is to use the actual E_{t-1} observed in period t-1. Replacing $\hat{E}_t$ by E_{t-1} in equation (2.1) would yield a measure of uncertainty:

$$RMSPE = 100\sqrt{\frac{1}{T}\sum_{t=1}^{T}\left(\frac{E_t - E_{t-1}}{E}\right)^2}$$ (2.2)

We can also use the standard deviation as a predictor of $\hat{E}_t$, by denoting the mean as $\bar{E}$ and substituting it for $\hat{E}_t$ in equation (2.1) thus:

$$SD = \sqrt{\frac{1}{T-1}\sum_{t=1}^{T}(E_t - E)^2}$$ (2.3)

The standard deviation method is, however, scale dependent. A closely related method which is not scale dependent is the percentage coefficient of variation:

$$CV = 100\frac{1}{E}\sqrt{\frac{1}{T-1}\sum_{t=1}^{T}(E_t - E)^2}$$ (2.4)

The above models of uncertainty can be regarded as assuming σ_t to be small for all time t. In the literature, these measures of volatility are referred to as time invariant measures. Since the actual variance of stock returns are widely acknowledged to be time varying, the usefulness of time invariant measures in measuring risk has been questioned. It is therefore, more appropriate that σ_t should be seen as varying over time and dependent on past values of $\sigma_{t-1}, \sigma_{t-2}$, etc. This has led to increasing attempts to develop more acceptable measures such as time varying measures of volatility.

Modeling Volatility

According to Engle (1993), financial market volatility is predictable. In principle this claim may only be justified when ARCH effects are present. The implication of this observation for risk averse investors is that they can adjust their portfolios by reducing their commitments to assets whose volatilities are predicted to increase, thereby reducing their exposure to risk. Predicting volatility is really just a prediction of variance, a prediction that the potential size of a price move is small or great. Volatility forecasting is an imprecise activity, just like predicting rain. You can be correct in predicting the probability of rain, but still have no rain.

15

In modeling volatility, time series statistics are used to find the best forecast of volatility. By using time series statistics it is possible to determine whether recent information is more important than old information and how fast information decays. We can determine whether volatility is equally sensitive to market up moves as it is to down moves, and whether the size of past returns is proportional to the magnitude of volatility experienced today.

ARCH Models

The most important development in modelling volatility changes was the *autoregressive conditional heteroskedasticity* or ARCH model, introduced by Engle (1982). The growth rate of the ARCH literature has been truly spectacular over the last decade, so much as to evoke the following comment from Bera and Higgins (1993), 'The numerous applications of ARCH models defies observed trends in scientific advancement. Usually applications lag theoretical developments, but Engle's ARCH model ...... has been applied to numerous economic and financial data series of many countries, while it has seen relatively fewer theoretical advancements.' This growth has stemmed primarily from the versatility of ARCH models in capturing some important stylised facts of many economic and financial data. These include unconditional distributions have thick tails, variances change over time and large and (small) changes tend to be followed by large (small) changes of either sign. The ARCH model has been applied to test several asset pricing models such as the Capital Asset Pricing Model (CAPM) and the Arbitrage Pricing Model (APT) in order to capture the time varying systematic risk process of these models. In the CAPM, there is a direct association between variance and risk as well as a fundamental tradeoff relationship between risk and return. The ARCH-M developed by Engle, Lilien and Robins (1987) [discussed below) provides a useful tool for estimating this linear relationship.

ARCH models have been used to examine how information flows across countries, markets and assets, to develop optimal hedging strategies. In macroeconomics, ARCH techniques have been used to model the relationship between the time-varying conditional variance and the risk premia in the term structure of interest rates. In modelling exchange rate dynamics, international portfolio management depends on expected exchange rate movement through time. Additionally the impact of exchange rate movements on different macroeconomic variables requires an understanding of exchange rate dynamics. In the absence of any structural model that captures these dynamics, the linear GARCH (p, q) model has been widely used for modelling exchange rate dynamics. ARCH models have also been used to measure inflation uncertainty, to study the effects of central bank intervention, and to characterise the relationship between the macroeconomy and the stock market. Before we describe the original ARCH model of Engle (1982) and subsequent extensions to the basic

ARCH model, we first outline the steps involved in measuring the volatility of asset returns.

Engle (1982, 1983) found in analysing results from models of inflation that large and small forecast errors appeared to occur in clusters. This suggested a form of heteroscedasticity in which the variance of the forecast error depends on the size of the preceding disturbance. The ARCH models discussed below all exploit a common statistical characteristic referred to as *conditional* variance. The conditional mean uses information from the previous period and is in general a random variable, depending on the information set F_{t-1} and is given by:

$$m_t \equiv E[y_t|F_{t-1}] \equiv E_{t-1}[y_t] \qquad (2.5)$$

where y_t is the rate of return of a particular stock or market portfolio from time t-1 to t, F_{t-1} is the past information set containing the realised values of all relevant variables up to time t-1, and E is the mathematical expectations operator. Since investors know the information in F_{t-1} when making their investment decision at time t, the relevant expected return and volatility to the investors are in turn given by the conditional expected value of y_t, represented in (2.5) above and the *conditional variance* of y_t, given F_{t-1}, represented by equation (2.6) below;

$$\sigma_t^2 \equiv E_{t-1}[y_t - m_t]^2 . \qquad (2.6)$$

Since volatility measures the variability of returns, investors will forecast more accurately by using the *conditional variance*, σ_t^2, since it depends on the information set F_{t-1}.

To analyse the returns y_t on an asset received in period t, we need to follow three basic steps: (1) specify m_t; (2) specify σ_t^2; and (3) specify the density function of ε^2. In financial markets, m_t is generally designated as the risk premium, or the expected return which is frequently set at zero, at least for high-frequency data. Regarding the specification of the density function, the characteristics of stock returns which tend to exhibit nonnormal unconditional sampling distributions will be examined at various points particularly when we investigate the application of ARCH to stock return data. Interestingly, according to Engle and Gonzalez-Rivera (1991) the assumption that the conditional density is normally distributed usually does not appreciably affect the estimates even if it is false. In presenting the various models examined below we will focus mostly on *Step 2*. In particular, we examine how the conditional variances depend on past information. Equation (2.6) is also used to determine time varying risk premiums and to forecast volatility. There will be little discussion on the estimation procedures, since these have been dealt with elsewhere (see Engle 1982; Bollerslev 1986; and Hamilton 1994). Suffice it to say that maximum-

17

likelihood estimation is generally recommended and used and that the likelihood function typically assumes that the conditional density is Gaussian.

The Linear ARCH(p) Model

ARCH can be defined in terms of the distribution of the errors of a dynamic linear regression model. Assume we are required to estimate y_t, the rate of return, on a particular stock in the following linear regression model

$$y_t = x_t' \xi + \varepsilon_t, \qquad t = 1, \ldots, T, \qquad (2.7)$$

where x_t is a k × 1 vector of exogenous variables, including lagged values of the dependent variable, and ξ is a k × 1 vector of regression parameters. The ARCH model characterises the distribution of the stochastic error ε_t conditional on the realised values of the set of variables $\{y_{t-1}, x_{t-1}, y_{t-2}, x_{t-2}, \ldots\}$. Engle's (1982) insight was to set the conditional variance of a series of errors, ε_t's, as a function of lagged errors, time, parameters, and predetermined variables:

$$\sigma_t^2 = \sigma^2 (\varepsilon_{t-1}, \varepsilon_{t-2}, \ldots, t, \xi, b), \qquad (2.8)$$

$$\varepsilon_t = \sigma_t^2 Z_t, \qquad (2.9)$$

where $Z_t \sim$ i.i.d. with $E(Z_t) = 0$, $E(Z_t^2) = 1$. By definition, ε_t is serially uncorrelated with mean zero, but the conditional variance of ε_t equals σ_t^2, which may be changing through time.

Engle (1982) then chose a functional form for $\sigma_t^2 (\bullet)$:

$$\sigma_t^2 = \omega + \sum_{i=1}^{p} \alpha_i \varepsilon_{t-i}^2 \qquad (2.10)$$

where ω and $\{\alpha_i\}$, $i = 1$, p are nonnegative constants. This is necessary to keep σ_t^2 nonnegative. The distinguishing feature of this model is not that the conditional variance is a function of the conditioning set $\sigma^2 (\varepsilon_{t-1}, \varepsilon_{t-2}, \ldots, t, \xi, b)$, but rather it is the particular functional form that is specified. Episodes of volatility are generally characterised as the clustering of large shocks to the dependent variable. The conditional variance function is formulated to *mimic* this phenomenon. In the regression model, a large shock is represented by a large

18

deviation of y_t from its conditional mean m_t, or equivalently, a large positive or negative value of ε_t. In the ARCH regression model, the variance of the current error ε_t, conditional on the realised errors ε_{t-i}, is an increasing function of the magnitude of the lagged errors irrespective of their sign. Hence large errors of either sign tend to be followed by a large error of either sign, and similarly, small errors of either sign tend to be followed by small errors of either sign. The order for the lag p determines the length of time for which a shock persists in conditioning the variance of subsequent errors. The effect of a return shock i periods ago (i ≤ p) on current volatility is governed by the paramaters α_i in equation (2.10). Normally, the older the news, the less effect it has on current volatility. Investors choose different values of p, depending on how fast they think volatility is changing. Engle (1982) parameterised the conditional variance as (2.10) where the weights α_i decline linearly. The model in (2.10) is referred to as ARCH(p), in which the conditional variance is simply a weighted average of past squared forecast errors. This is the volatility estimate used by the vast majority of market participants.

The appeal of (2.10) lies in the way it captures the positive serial correlation in ε_t^2: a high value of ε_t^2 increases σ_{t+1}^2, which in turn increases the expectation of ε_{t+1}^2, and so on. In other words, a large (small) value of ε_t^2 tends to be followed by a large (small) value of ε_{t+1}^2. The advantage of the ARCH formulation is that these parameters can be estimated from historical data and used to forecast future patterns in volatility. The above equation (2.10) can be written as:

$$\varepsilon_t^2 = \omega + \sum_{i=1}^{p} \alpha_i \varepsilon_{t-i}^2 + \left[\varepsilon_t^2 - \sigma_t^2 \right] \qquad (2.11)$$

where the term in brackets is unforecastable and is considered to be the innovation in the autoregression for ε^2. It is a simple procedure to test whether the residuals ε_t from a regression model exhibit time-varying heteroscedasticity. Engle (1982) derived a test based on the Lagrange Multiplier (LM) principle. An LM test for $\alpha_1 = ... = \alpha_p = 0$ can be calculated as TR^2 from the regression of ε_t^2 on $\varepsilon_{t-1}^2 ...... \varepsilon_{t-p}^2$, where T denotes the sample size.[4]

GARCH

Bollerslev (1986) extended the ARCH model into GARCH i.e., Generalised ARCH. The innovation here is that GARCH allows past conditional variances to enter equations (2.9) and (2.10). The intention of GARCH is that it can parsimoniously represent a higher order ARCH process. The GARCH (p, q) can be represented as follows:

$$\sigma_t^2 = \omega + \sum_{i=1}^{p} \alpha_i \varepsilon_{t-i}^2 + \sum_{i=1}^{q} \beta i \sigma_{t-i}^2 \qquad (2.12)$$

σ_t^2 is a function of lagged values of ε_t^2 and $\omega, \{\alpha_i\}, i = 1, p,$ and $\{\beta_i\}, q$ are nonnegative constants. As indicated in (2.12), GARCH models explain variance by two distributed lags, one on past squared residuals to capture high frequency effects, and the second on lagged values of the variance itself, to capture longer term influences. An appealing feature of the GARCH (p, q) model concerns the time series dependence in ε_t^2.

Equation (2.12) can be written as:

$$\varepsilon_t^2 = \omega + \sum_{i=1}^{p} (\alpha_i + \beta_i) \varepsilon_{t-i}^2 - \sum_{i=1}^{p} \beta_i \left[\varepsilon_{t-i}^2 - \sigma_{t-i}^2 \right] + \left[\varepsilon_t^2 - \sigma_{t-i}^2 \right] \qquad (2.13)$$

Equation (2.13) shows that ε^2 follows an autoregressive moving average (ARMA) process. A systematic approach to estimation is maximum likelihood. This involves postulating a well defined objective function and then maximising it with respect to the unknown parameters. As the objective function is not quadratic, iterative algorithms are required. Various algorithms have been used but the GARCH (1, 1), estimation is rather well behaved. This is simplest of the GARCH models and can be expressed as:

$$\sigma_t^2 = \omega + \alpha \varepsilon_{t-1}^2 + \beta \sigma_{t-1}^2 = \frac{\omega}{(1-\beta)} + \alpha \sum_{i=0}^{\infty} \beta^i \varepsilon_{t-i-1}^2 \qquad (2.14)$$

The GARCH (1, 1) in equation (2.14) embodies a very intuitive forecasting strategy: the variance expected at any given date is a combination of a long run variance and the variance expected for the last period, adjusted to take into account the size of last period's observed shock. In the GARCH (1, 1) model, the effect of a return shock on current volatility declines geometrically over time. Despite the success of both ARCH and GARCH models (see the survey by Bollerslev et al (1992)) these models cannot capture some important features of financial and economic data. The most interesting feature not addressed by these models is the leverage or asymmetric effect (discussed below) discovered by Black (1976), and confirmed by Nelson (1990) and Schwert (1990), among others. Mandelbrot (1963) and Fama (1965) were amongst the first to observe that unconditional price or stock returns tend to have fatter tails than a normal distribution exhibits, in the form of skewness[5] but more pronounced in the form of excess kurtosis. For example in the GARCH (p, q) model examined in (2.4.3) above, the unconditional distribution of the ε_ts have fatter tails than the normal distribution. Baillie and DeGennaro (1990) and de Jong et al (1990) assumed conditionally t-distributed errors (the conditional t-distribution allows for heavier tails than the normal distribution) in a GARCH (1, 1) model for the conditional variance, and found that failure to model the fat-tailed properties leads to spurious results in terms of the estimated risk-return tradeoff. One solution to the kurtosis problem is the adoption of conditional distributions with fatter tails than the normal distribution. Nelson's (1991) EGARCH (discussed below) represents one of the more successful attempts to model excess conditional kurtosis in stock return indices based on a generalised exponential distribution.

EGARCH

In the case of the GARCH models discussed above, we squared the residuals before estimating them. However, it is possible that up and down moves do not have the same predictability for future volatility. Nelson (1991) was the first investigator to model leverage effects, (i.e. where the down moves are more influential for predicting volatility than up moves), by introducing the exponential ARCH or EGARCH model which can be represented as follows:

$$\log \sigma_t^2 = \omega + \sum_{i=1}^{p} \beta_i \log \sigma_{t-i}^2 + \sum_{i=1}^{p} \alpha_i |\varepsilon_{t-i}| / \sigma_{t-i}^{2\,1/2}$$

$$+ \sum_{i=1}^{p} \gamma_i \varepsilon_{t-i} / \sigma_{t-i}^{2\,1/2} \tag{2.15}$$

The EGARCH model was largely motivated by Black's (1976) empirical observation that stock volatility tends to rise following negative returns and to drop following positive returns. The EGARCH model exploits this empirical regularity by making the conditional variance estimate a function of both the size and the sign of lagged residuals. Unlike the linear GARCH (p, q) model, the EGARCH model places no restrictions on the parameters α_i and β_i to ensure nonnegativity of the conditional variances. Equation (2.15) allows positive and negative values of ε_t to have different impacts on volatility. The EGARCH model is asymmetric because the level $\varepsilon_{t-i} / \sigma_{t-i}^{2\,1/2}$ is included with coefficient γ_i. Since this coefficient is typically negative, positive return shocks generate less volatility than negative return shocks, all else being equal. In summary the EGARCH model differs from the standard GARCH model in two main respects: *firstly,* the EGARCH model allows good news and bad news to have a different impact on volatility, while the standard GARCH does not, and *secondly,* the EGARCH model allows big news to have a greater impact on volatility than the standard GARCH model.

The Taylor - Schwert Model

Davidian and Carroll (1987) argue that scale estimates based on *absolute* residuals are more robust to the presence of thick-tailed residuals than scale estimates based on squared residuals. Schwert (1989) applied the Davidian and Carroll intuition to ARCH models, conjecturing that estimating σ_t^2 with the square of a distributed lag of absolute residuals (as opposed to estimating it with a distributed lag of squared residuals, as in GARCH) would be more robust to innovations in x, i.e. ε_x 's with thick tailed distributions. Taylor (1986) proposed a similar method. Generally, since thick-tailed standarised residuals are the norm in empirical applications of ARCH (see Bollerslev et al., 1992), the use of absolute residuals as opposed to squared residuals in estimating time varying volatilities in asset returns is more appropriate.

Schwert's (1989) model produces monthly volatility estimates from monthly return data. The measure is more robust than the standard deviation measure because of its insensitivity to extreme values, the measure being based on absolute deviations of returns from its conditional mean. Schwert's method for estimating volatility is calculated by first regressing monthly returns on 12 monthly dummy variables and 12 lagged return values,

$$\sigma_t^x = \beta_1(H)\sigma_t^x + \sum_{m=1}^{12} \beta_m SD_{m,t} + \varepsilon_{2,t}^x \qquad (2.16)$$

where $\beta_1(H)$ is a 12th order polynomial in the lag operator H, the SD_m 's are monthly dummy variables to capture seasonal variations in the means and standard deviations of the variables, and the σ_t^x are innovations which are obtained as the absolute values of the residuals from the following equation, i.e., $\sigma_t^x = /\varepsilon_{1,t}^x/$ where,

$$\varepsilon_{1,t}^x = \Delta Log(X)_t - E_t(\Delta Log(X)_t / I_{t-1})$$

$$= \Delta Log(X)_t - \alpha_1(H)\Delta Log(X)_t - \sum_{m=1}^{12} \alpha_m SD_{m,t} \quad (2.17)$$

and $\alpha_1(H)$ is another 12th order polynomial in the lag operator H. The measure of conditional volatility in equation (2.16) represents a generalisation of the 12-month rolling standard estimator used by Officer (1973), Fama (1976) and Merton (1980) to measure stock market volatility, because it allows the conditional mean to vary over time in equation (2.17) while also allowing different weights to apply to the lagged absolute unpredicted changes in stock market returns in equation (2.16). This measure has been used by Schwert (1989) to examine the relationship between stock market volatility and underlying economic volatility, and more recently by Koutoulas and Kryzanowski (1996) to examine the role of conditional macroeconomic factors in an arbitrage pricing model and in Chapters four and five of this thesis, where the Schwert (1989) measure is used to examine the relationship between stock market volatility and several financial and macroeconomic variables for Australia.[6]

Higgins and Bera (1992) nested GARCH and the Taylor-Schwert model in a class of 'NARCH' (nonlinear ARCH) models, which set $\hat{\sigma}_t^{2\sigma}$ equal to a distributed lag of past absolute residuals each raised to the 2σ power. The chief appeal of NARCH is that it is more robust to conditionally thick-tailed $\varepsilon_x's$ than GARCH. NARCH limits the influence of large residuals essentially the same way as the estimators employed in the robust statistics literature e.g. Davadian and Carroll, (1987).

ARCH-M

Assets with high expected risk must offer a high rate of return to induce investors to hold them. In this case, increases in conditional variance should be associated with increases in the conditional mean. Merton (1980) derives an equation that relates the expected return on the market linearly to the conditional variance of the market:

$$m_t = \delta\sigma_t^2 \tag{2.18}$$

where δ can be interpreted as the coefficient of the relative risk aversion of an agent, and m is interpreted as a time-varying risk premium that is, the increase in the expected rate of return due to an increase in the variance of the return. Engle, Lilien and Robins (1987) propose the ARCH-M or GARCH-M which incorporates an equation like (2.18) in which the conditional mean is an explicit function of the conditional variance:

$$y_t = g\left(x_{t-1}, \sigma_t^2; b\right) + \varepsilon_t \tag{2.19}$$

In (2.19), an increase in the conditional variance will be associated with an increase or a decrease in the conditional mean of y_t depending on the sign of the partial derivative of $g\left(x_{t-1}, \sigma_t^2; b\right)_t$ with respect to σ_t^2. ARCH-M models have been frequently used in finance where many theories involve an explicit tradeoff between the risk and the expected return; ARCH-M is suited to modelling this relationship due to the observation that the variance may frequently be time-varying.

MARCH

Friedman and Laibson (1989) argue that stock movements have "ordinary" and "extraordinary" components. This motivated their modified ARCH (MARCH) model, which bounds g($\bullet$) in (2.20) to keep the "extraordinary" component from being too influential in determining $\hat{\sigma}_t^2$. The MARCH model can be represented as:

$$\hat{\sigma}_{t+h}^2 = \omega h + \beta_h \hat{\sigma}_t^2 + h^{1/2} g\left(\hat{\varepsilon}_x\right), \qquad (2.20)$$

$$\text{where } g\left(\hat{\varepsilon}_x\right) \equiv \alpha > 0 \text{ if } \gamma \hat{\varepsilon}_x^2 \geq \pi / 2$$

$$\equiv \alpha \sin\left[\gamma \hat{\varepsilon}_x^2\right] \text{ if } \gamma \hat{\varepsilon}_x^2 < \pi / 2.$$

This model can be understood intuitively if we assume that ε_x has occasional large outliers. Least-squares based procedures such as GARCH will not estimate σ_t^2 efficiently. In accord with Friedman and Laibson's (1989) intuition, the thicker tailed the conditional distribution of ε_x, the less weight should be given to 'large' observations. The point of the MARCH model is to enable the ARCH mechanism to focus on the ordinary component of stock returns by de-emphasising the extraordinary events. In essence, the estimated MARCH model distinguishes the extraordinary movements and removes most of their impact, and then analyses the persistence in volatility of the remaining ordinary component. Results from the estimated MARCH model show that extremely high volatility levels such as the October 1987 crash decay quickly, while only marginally high volatility levels decay much more slowly.

Multivariate ARCH Models

Since economic variables are interrelated, many issues in asset pricing and portfolio decisions can only be meaningfully examined in a multivariate context. Estimating some financial coefficients such as systematic risk (beta coefficients) and hedge ratios, require the sample values of covariance between relevant variables. A general definition of multivariate ARCH can be represented as follows:

24

$$\varepsilon_t = z_t \Omega_t^{1/2}, \qquad\qquad (2.21)$$

where z_t is i.i.d., $E(z_t) = 0$, $\text{var}(z_t) = 1$, $\{\varepsilon_t\}$ denotes an $N \times 1$ vector stochastic process, and Ω is the time-varying $N \times N$ covariance matrix which is positive definite and measurable with respect to time $t - 1$ information set. The simplest multivariate ARCH model is that presented by Engle et al. (1990), in which certain linear combinations of the observable X_t's drive the conditional covariance matrix. Inference in the multivariate ARCH model is similar to the univariate model. A complete description of the properties and parameterisation of multivariate ARCH is given in Higgins and Bera (1993).

Several studies (e.g. Domiwitz and Hakkio (1985); Diebold and Pauly (1988a) and Baillie and Bollerslev (1990)) have found the weak results in the foreign exchange market using univariate ARCH-M models to estimate time-varying risk premia. Some have speculated that these results are due to the poor proxies for risk as given by the conditional variances. In particular, the above authors suggest that the premium might be better approximated by a function of the time varying cross-currency conditional covariance's and not just the own conditional variance. Lee (1988) found support for this hypothesis, in that the conditional covariance between the German Mark and the Yen/US dollar spot rates (modelled by the bivariate ARCH (12) model) helps explain the weekly movements in the Yen/U.S. dollar rate.

Multivariate ARCH models have also addressed various policy issues related to the foreign exchange market. Recent studies by Diebold and Pauly (1988b) and Bollerslev (1986) examine the effect on short-run exchange rate volatility following the creation of the European Monetary System (EMS). In all these cases it was found that an increase in the conditional variances and covariance's among the different European rates occurred after those currencies joined the EMS. More recently several papers have investigated the effect of central bank intervention on the foreign exchange rate dynamics in the context of a multivariate GARCH model. For example Connolly and Taylor (1990), Mundaca (1990) and Humpage and Osterbert (1990) come to the conclusion that a positive correlation between current intervention and exchange rate volatility exists in all cases.

Sources of ARCH

An important characteristic of the ARCH process which makes it suitable for modelling financial and economic series is the assumption of the lack of serial correlation in the distribution of the unconditional variance of the errors, where σ^2 is a constant. Since the efficient market hypothesis asserts that past rates of return can not be used to improve the prediction of future rates of return, it is important to confirm that the presence of ARCH does not represent a violation of market efficiency. This lack of serial correlation does not, however, imply that the ε_ts are independent. A major contribution of the ARCH literature is the finding that apparent changes in the volatility of economic time series may be predictable and result from a specific type of nonlinear dependence rather than exogenous structural change in the variance. Using U.S. daily stock return data, Lamoureux and Lastrapes (1990) provide empirical support of the hypothesis that ARCH is a manifestation of the time dependence in the rate of information arrival to the market. They assume that I_t the number of times new information comes to the market in period t, is serially correlated. Since I_t is not observable, Lamoureux and Lastrapes used daily trading volume, V_t, as a proxy for the daily information that flows into the market. When V_t is included as an extra variable in the GARCH (1, 1) model (2.14), its coefficient was highly significant for all of the 20 stocks they considered. Furthermore when V_t is included in (2.14) this made the ARCH effects (coefficients α_1 and β_1) become negligible for most of the stocks. In summary, an important property of speculative prices is serial correlation in the second moments, a search for the causes of this serial correlation has only recently begun. One possible explanation for the prominence of ARCH effects is the presence of a serially correlated news arrival process as evidenced by Lamoureux and Lastrapes (1990), Diebold and Nerlove (1989) and Gallant, Hsieh and Tauchen (1991). This empirical work supports the view that ARCH in daily stock returns is an outcome of the time dependence in the news that flows into the market.

Closely related to searching for ARCH effects is interest in how persistent are shocks to the volatility process, that is once volatility increases, for how long does it remain high? Persistence of volatility has implications for the value of the parameters of the various models presented above. In the linear GARCH (p, q) in (2.12), persistence is manifested when α_1 and $\beta_1 = 1$. Engle and Bollerslev (1986) refer to this class of models as integrated in variance, or IGARCH. In an IGARCH process, a current shock persists indefinitely in conditioning the future variances. The regular occurrence of vary large persistence in financial time series data is not theoretically justified. However, Kearns and Pagan (1993) feel safe in concluding that there is persistence of shocks in volatility, and this persistence is as true of small shocks as it is of large ones. Moreover, they claim that there is no evidence that persistence is due to structural change, since over long periods of time, persistence has remained constant.

Comparing Alternative Volatility Models

In comparing alternative ARCH models, a number of approaches can be taken. Nelson and Foster's (1994) research on ARCH models concentrates on refining techniques which approximate the measurement accuracy of ARCH conditional variance estimates and on comparing the efficiency achieved by different ARCH models. By deriving the asymptotic distribution of the measurement error, Nelson and Foster (1994) are able to characterise the relative importance of different kinds of misspecification. In particular, they show that misspecifying conditional means adds only trivially to measurement error, while other factors (for example capturing the 'leverage effect', accommodating thick-tailed residuals, and correctly modelling the variability of the conditional variance process) are potentially much more important.

Another approach involves an examination of how well different models of heteroscedasticity measure the value of ε_t^2. Pagan and Schwert (1990) fitted several models to monthly U.S. stock returns from 1834 to 1925. They found that the EGARCH model of Nelson performed best overall in both in-sample and out-of-sample cases. A related approach involves calculating various specification tests of the fitted model. Higgins and Bera (1992) used the LM test whilst Nelson (1991) used moments tests and analysis of outliers. Yet another approach by Engle and Mustafa (1992) uses an approach based on the usefulness of a given specification of the conditional variance of the observed prices of stock options. Options give investors the right to buy or sell the security at some date in the future at a price agreed upon today. The value of the option increases with the perceived variability of the security. By assuming that stock prices can be approximated by a normal distribution with constant variance, the Black and Scholes (1973) formula which relates the price of the option to investors perception of the variance of the stock price can be used to value the option. These option prices can then be used to construct the market's perception of conditional variance which can be compared to the series implied by a given time series model. The results of such a comparison suggests that GARCH (1, 1) and EGARCH (1, 1) models can improve on the market's assessment of the conditional variance of stock prices.

ARCH models have been criticised for being *ad hoc* i.e., while they have been successful in empirical applications, they are *statistical* models, not *economic* models [Campbell and Hentschel (1993) and Andersen (1992)]. However, these comments are based partly, perhaps, wholly on the observation that given the variety of ARCH models from which to choose. How do researchers choose between them? Nelson and Foster (1994) suggest that the robustness results of Davidian and Carroll (1987) hold in the ARCH context. In particular, EGARCH and Taylor-Schwert are more robust than GARCH to conditionally thick-tailed ε_t s, (i.e. scale estimates based on absolute residuals are more robust to the presence of thick-tailed residuals than scale estimates based on squared residuals). This indicates a preference to design ARCH models to be robust to thick-tailed ε_t s , since conditional leptokurtosis seems to be the rule in financial applications of ARCH.

Forecasting Volatility

The measurement of *ex ante* financial asset return volatility is extremely important for all participants in the markets. A commonly used approach to forecasting volatility involves using the market price of stock options. This method uses the market prices of contingent claims to work out the implied volatility. Here, a theoretical pricing function is used to relate the price of a contingent claim to the volatility of the underlying asset and solve it for the implied volatility given by the market price of the asset. Latane and Rendleman (1976) suggested computing volatility from the Black-Scholes option pricing formula. Implied volatility can be computed from this formula by calculating the implied standard deviation (ISD), assuming that the volatility remains constant over the life of the option. However, the problem with this approach is that the true volatility must be constant, which is more likely if the term over which the option applies is sufficiently short such that stock prices can be considered to approximate a normal distribution with constant variance. If this is not the case then the interpretation of volatility calculated by the ISD is unclear.

The Black-Scholes Model

Theoretical and empirical research on security prices since the 1950s has largely supported the 'efficient markets' of the "random walk" model. In an efficient market, asset price movements can be described by an equation like (2.22).

$$r_t = \frac{S_t - S_{t-1}}{S_{t-1}} = \mu_t + \varepsilon_t; \quad E[\varepsilon_t] = 0, Var[\varepsilon_t] = \sigma_t^2 \quad (2.22)$$

The return at time t, r_t, is the percentage change in the asset price S over the period from t-1 to t. This is equal to μ_t, a random mean return for period t, plus a zero mean disturbance term ε_t, that is independent of all past and future $\varepsilon's$ It is the lack of serial correlation in the random $\varepsilon's$ that is the defining characteristic of efficient market pricing; past price movements give no information about the sign of the random component of return in period t. If S follows a random walk, the expected value of the return is zero and the variance of the random component is constant over-time. Thus, μ_t would have to be zero and the variance of the $\varepsilon's$ would be the same for all dates.

In deriving the option pricing formula, Black and Scholes (1972) needed to model stock price movements over very short intervals of time. The formulation they adopted is an extension of the random walk model to continuous time. The result is the lognormal diffusion model shown in (2.23).

$$\frac{dS}{S} = \mu\,dt + \sigma\,dz \qquad (2.23)$$

where dS is the asset price change over an infinitesimal time interval dt, μ is the mean return at an annual rate, dz is a time independent random disturbance with mean 0, variance is 1.dt (a stochastic process known as Brownian motion), and σ is the volatility, i.e. the standard deviation of the annual return. This model produces (continuously compounded) returns that follow a normal distribution and asset prices that have a lognormal distribution (i.e. the logarithm of S has a normal distribution). This implies that the cumulative return over a finite holding period of length T has expected value = μT, variance = $\sigma^2 T$ and standard deviation = $\sigma\sqrt{T}$.

An interesting feature of this asset price process is that with a constant volatility, the standard deviation, σ, of total returns over a holding period increases with the square root of the length of the period. This model, and subsequent extensions of it, have become the standard way to model asset price behavior. Empirical evidence shows that the behavior of asset returns in the real world differs fundamentally from (2.22) and (2.23). The following are the main differences. Volatility changes randomly over time. Prices in actual security markets are not perfectly uncorrelated over time. Positive correlation between consecutive price changes lowers (raises) measured volatility relative to the true value that should be used for σ. Observed price changes deviate consistently from lognormality. There are more very large changes and (consequently) more very small ones than a lognormal distribution calls for. The commonly used term for this is 'fat tails'. There is more weight in the tails of the actual returns distribution than in a lognormal distribution with the same variance.

The above discussion brings out one of the internal contradictions that are pervasive in applying theoretical derivative pricing models in practice. Volatility is known to be time-varying and stochastic, so a variety of methods to forecast it and to manage volatility risk are in use. Nevertheless, options are almost always priced simply by computing a point forecast for the unknown volatility and putting it into a constant volatility pricing model like Black-Scholes.

Computing Historical Volatility

Black and Scholes (1972) derived their option valuation equation under the assumption that stock returns followed a logarithmic diffusion process in continuous time with constant drift and volatility parameters as shown in equation (2.23).

Starting from an initial value S_0, the return, R, over the non-infinitesimal period from 0 to T is given by

$$R = \ln(S_T/S_0)$$

and R has a normal distribution, with

$$\text{Mean} = (\mu - \sigma^2/2)T \qquad (2.24)$$

$$\text{Standard deviation} = \sigma\sqrt{T}.$$

When an asset's price follows the constant volatility lognormal diffusion model of equation (2.23), σ can be estimated from historical data. The difficulty is that actual prices do not follow (2.23) exactly, so that price behavior may change over time and differ over intervals of different lengths. However, the ways in which (2.23) fails in practice are not established and regular enough for an alternative model to have become widely accepted. It is common, therefore, to compute volatility using historical price data as if (2.23) were correct, but to adjust the estimation methodology, or the volatility number it produces, in order to offset known or suspected problems. The resulting point estimate for σ then becomes the volatility input to the Black-Scholes model or another fixed volatility equation. Black-Scholes is familiar and easier to manipulate than any valuation model that adjusts for random volatility formally.

Estimating historical volatility and projecting it forward is a very common approach to volatility forecasting in practice. Consider a set of historical prices $\{S_0, S_1, \ldots S_T\}$, for some underlying asset that follows the process defined in equation (2.23). The first step is to compute the log price relatives, i.e., the percentage price changes expressed as continuously compounded rates $Rt = \ln(S_t/S_{t-1})$, for t from 1 to T. The estimate of the (constant) mean μ of R_t is the simple average

$$\bar{R} = \frac{\sum Rt}{T}. \qquad (2.25)$$

The variance of the R_t is given by

$$V^2 = \frac{\sum(Rt - \bar{R})}{(T-1)}. \qquad (2.26)$$

Annualizing the variance by multiplying by N, the number of price observations in a year and taking the square root yields the volatility,

$$\sigma = \sqrt{Nv^2}. \qquad (2.27)$$

Given that the constant parameter diffusion model of (2.23) is correct, the above procedure gives the best estimate of volatility that can be obtained from the available price data.

Estimating Volatility in Practice

In reality, several problems exist in attempting to measure volatility. Volatility clearly changes with time. The value of using all available data is severely limited by the fact that prices and returns for many securities appear to have some serial correlation and other distortions at both short and long intervals. Positive autocorrelation in returns will reduce estimated volatility. To limit the effect of serial correlation at high frequencies, researchers can estimate using fewer data points, but this may increase sampling error. Another way in which actual security returns differ from equation (2.24) is the well-documented problem of 'fat-tails'. Equities and many other securities exhibit more large price changes than is consistent with the lognormal diffusion model. Allowing for the fact that securities prices do not come from a constant volatility lognormal diffusion process, computing historical volatility as shown in equations (2.25 - 2.27) is no longer theoretically optimal. But many academic researchers and practitioners typically ignore them and calculate historical volatility estimates by the most basic method. The most common method of producing volatility forecasts from historical data is simply to select a sampling interval and the number of past prices to include in the calculation and then to apply equations (2.25 - 2.27).

Above we examined several extensions to the basic ARCH model of Engle. The complexity of these models is in part due to the training of financial economists and practitioners in classical statistics. While the estimation procedures greatly influence the kinds of models and procedures used to tackle quantitative problems in their specialist fields, the complexities involved with measuring volatility warrant equally sophisticated models to estimate volatility. However, on this point Figlewski (1996), has argued that the classical statistics' view of the world does not accurately represent the nature of the underlying structure of a financial market. In particular those trained in classical statistics tend to build models that are too complex and expect too much from them.

Figlewski (1996) illustrates this with an example. If it is assumed that *estimation and forecasting* are very similar to each other, goodness of fit statistics tell us how closely a model fits the data that was used in estimating it. However it is here that the classical statistics framework fundamentally misrepresents the nature of a financial market and leads those who adopt it to expect much better forecasting performance than can be achieved in practice. Consider the following estimation and prediction problem. Suppose we wanted to predict the movement of a whale, based on observing it over a period of time. The whale, being a large animal, should move with a fairly predictable pattern over the short run simply

31

from extrapolation. However, we do not think of a whale as following a fixed and immutable pattern, or one that we could ever hope to understand completely. The whale's behavior as a complex living organism must remain partially unpredictable no matter how much past data we may have. In this case, we are not looking at a fixed structure with constant but unknown parameters, but rather at a system that evolves over time, and perhaps alters its behavior rapidly on occasion. Because its evolution is partly stochastic, no amount of past data will allow us to know the exact structure of the system now or in the future. Prediction is possible only because the system evolves slowly and therefore our accumulated information from observing it decays only slowly. In this case, there may be an enormous difference between how well a model *fits in-sample* and how well it can *forecast out-of-sample*, and classical goodness of fit statistics may give little guidance about the latter. Also, having a large data sample for estimation does not guarantee that accurate parameter values can be computed. In any case, expanding the estimation data set by adding observations from the distant past can easily make the estimates of the current state of the system worse rather than better. In summary therefore, the more detailed and elaborate a model is, the better the fit one is generally able to obtain *in-sample*, but the faster the model tends to go off track when it is taken *out-of-sample*. Forecasting is a very different operation from in-sample estimation. In particular, financial markets behave very much like a whale. Nonetheless, it may be said that historical volatility computed over the recent periods provides the most accurate forecast for both long and short-run horizons.

Summary and Conclusions

ARCH models have been widely applied in economics and finance. In a recent survey by Bollerslev et al. (1992) more than 200 papers are cited applying ARCH and related models to financial time series. The vast majority of this work has focused on *in-sample* explanations of variance movements, rather than *forecasting per se*.

The majority of asset pricing theories relate expected returns on assets to their conditional variances and covariances. Since conditional variances and covariances are not observable, researchers have to estimate conditional second moments relying on models. An important concern is the accuracy of these models and how researchers may estimate them more accurately. In this chapter, various measures of volatility have been examined ranging from time invariant to time variant measures. In the former case one of the simplest measures examined was the standard deviation. A weakness of this measure is the assumption that volatility is constant, this being due to the standard deviation of returns increasing with the square root of the length of the period. Empirical evidence, however, shows us that the behaviour of asset returns in the real world changes randomly over time. This led us to an examination of time variant models for measuring volatility.

The ARCH model of Engle (1982) allowing the current variance σ_t^2 to be determined by both a long-term constant component and a short-term varying component. Since ARCH models are characterised by specifying conditional first and second moments of asset returns, their use in modelling volatility has been popularised by variants of this model. The ARCH (p) model allows one to account for volatility clustering which, in turn, tells us something about the predictability of volatility. The extension of ARCH to GARCH facilitated the entry of past conditional variances into the ARCH model. The simplest GARCH model examined, GARCH (1,1), appeals in that the variance expected at any given date is a combination of long run variance and the variance expected for the last period, adjusted to take into account the size of last period's observed shock. We noted that despite the empirical success of both ARCH and GARCH, these models failed to capture some interesting features of stock returns such as the leverage effect. The introduction of the EGARCH model by Nelson (1991) provided for this, by placing a bigger coefficient on squared residuals when they are negative than when they are positive.

In a study by Pagan and Schwert (1990), EGARCH was found to be a better predictor in both in-sample and out of sample forecasting performance than GARCH. Finally, we noted that the Davadian and Carroll (1987) intuition that scale estimates based on absolute residuals (e.g. Taylor-Schwert model) appears to be more robust to the presence of thick-tailed residuals than scale estimates based on squared residuals is widely supported in the literature. In conclusion, the task of any model is to describe the typical historical pattern of volatility and use this to forecast future episodes. In doing so, we noted that the researcher is drawn toward constructing very complex models which typically provide a better in-sample fit than when taken out-of-sample. It is therefore intriguing to know how some of the above models perform when they are applied to measuring volatility, since this is an all important step towards examining the effects of financial asset volatility on real economic activity.

3 Financial Volatility and Real Economic Activity

Introduction

The rationale for studying the relationship between financial and real economic activity arises from both theoretical models and empirical evidence which indicates that movements in financial asset prices are potentially important for understanding how the economy behaves. Failing to take account of the fact that extraordinary movements in financial asset prices have occurred from time to time in the past and can occur at any time in the future would therefore be a serious omission. Recent changes to the financial sector, particularly the deregulation of financial markets, has made the study of the inter-relationship between financial volatility and real economic activity more urgent. Since financial liberalisation began in the 1970s and 1980s and a universal expansion of equity markets has taken place in both developed and developing economies. Whether this phenomenal growth in stock markets affects real economic activity depends to some extent on the degree of volatility which stock markets exhibit. Keynes (1964) and Singh (1993) believe that highly volatile markets appear to induce short-term speculative investment practices which may lead to reductions in real-sector investment activities. These inturn may induce broader macroeconomic instability. Furthermore, increasing financial market volatility may have deleterious effects on the macroeconomy via increasing financial fragility. In general, the literature on financial economics appears relatively quiescent in regards to analysing the links between financial volatility and real economic activity. The objective of this chapter is to systematically explore these links.

The chapter provides an overview of the theoretical and empirical literature relevant to the issues examined in subsequent chapters of this book. Initially we explore the issue of stock market volatility by examining the relationship between stock market prices and fundamentals. This issue is subsequently examined further in Chapter four of the book, where an empirical model of the causes of stock market volatility in Australia is estimated. The Section titled 'Financial Instability and Macroeconomic Activity' examines the theory of financial instability and links to macroeconomic activity within Minsky's financial instability hypothesis. This is followed by a review of developing countries' experiences with financial liberalisation in an attempt to provide an insight into the relationship between financial volatility and real economic activity in lesser developed economies. In the final Section of this Chapter, we investigate the issue of monetary volatility and its effects on financial and non-financial activity, by providing an overview of monetary theory as well as examining the empirical evidence relating to the operation of monetary policy in Australia. This analysis provides a background to Chapters six and seven of this book, where some central aspects of the connection between financial activity and real economic activity are investigated.

Stock Market Volatility

Financial asset prices (stocks, bonds, foreign exchange and other investment assets) have shown significant changes in volatility over time. The stock market fall on October 19, 1987 was the biggest one day price change ever recorded in percentage terms. The Dow Jones Industrial (DJ) average fell 22.5 per cent in one day. More recently the DJ average recorded a rise of 25 percentage points over the two year period to March 1997. Changes in stock prices, as measured by the standard deviation of percentage changes in the nominal Standard and Poor's Composite Stock Price Index, from 1871 to 1987, shows the standard deviation of the 12 monthly stock price changes to have many years when stock volatility was as high as 1987. Schwert (1990) discovered after examining the highest and lowest daily returns to several broad stock market indexes over a 100 year period that an increase in stock market volatility brings an increased chance of large stock price changes of either sign. This observation was clearly demonstrated by the tendency for high and low returns to cluster in brief sub periods over the 1802-1989 period, indicating an increase in stock market volatility during these periods.

Volatility plays a fundamentally important role in determining stock market efficiency. The extent to which the stock market is efficient in the sense that it serves as an efficient mechanism for allocating resources is central to the modern private enterprise system.[7] Several studies[8] exist on this subject, covering specific aspects, such as variance-bounds tests for *excess* stock-price volatility.[9] Shiller (1981) and LeRoy and Porter (1981) were amongst the first to use variance bounds restrictions imposed by rational expectations to study the behaviour of US equity prices. Shiller calculated the sample variance of the ex post rational price series and compared it to the sample variance of the actual stock prices. He found that the actual stock prices have a variance that is many times larger than the variance of the ex post rational series he constructed, and he concluded that actual prices are too volatile when compared to the ex post rational price series to be consistent with the constant discount rate dividend valuation model and rational expectations. Shiller concluded that even allowing for time varying discount rates, this could not account for the observed *excess* volatility, and he stated that the likely cause of *excess* volatility is market inefficiency. The findings by Shiller and by LeRoy and Porter were viewed with skepticism in the academic finance profession, whose priors were centered on belief in efficient stock markets.

The *excess* volatility debate which began in the 1970s continues today, with evidence on the existence of *excess* stock price volatility and its implications for market efficiency being ambiguous. The debate today centres on varying dividend discount rates as an explanation for *excess* volatility. After an exhaustive review of the literature on *excess* volatility, Kupiec (1993) came to the conclusion that since the 'true' model of discount rates is unknown, the discount rate explanation cannot be rejected. However, if time-varying discount rates are an important source of volatility, in an efficient market we should expect these discount rates to react to changes in macroeconomic fundamentals that are *'news'* to the market participants. Changes in economic fundamentals should induce changes in discount rates, and dividend growth expectations, and thereby induce changes in stock prices.

Fundamentals and Stock Market Prices

Prices set in the stock market determine the actual cost of new capital for firms that issue shares, while also providing a measure of the opportunity cost of capital acquired through retained earnings. Prices set in the stock market are said to be efficient in the sense that they embody all available relevant information. Kupiec (1993) finds the evidence for stock market efficiency to be ambiguous, and shows that existing empirical evidence provides ample opportunity to support either the efficient market hypothesis or the alternative of market inefficiency.

Where markets are efficient, large changes in stock prices reflect large shifts in investors' rational expectations about future values of the fundamental economic variables that affect the valuation of common stocks. In criticising the efficient market hypothesis, LeRoy and Porter (1981), Shiller (1981) and later Flavin (1983), Kleidon (1986) and Marsh and Merton (1986) argue that financial markets may be too volatile to be accounted for by the efficient markets hypothesis.[10] O'Scott (1991) remarks that while economists have generally failed to explain either stock market movements or changes in stock market volatility over time, the models seemingly do work well for bond prices. O'Scott (1991) points to the presence of irrational or near-rational bubbles in the stock market as a possible reason for economists' inability to explain stock market volatility.

Whether markets reflect all relevant information in forming expectations that determine fundamental values is essentially asking the question, 'Is the market efficient?' If markets do not incorporate all relevant information in forming expectations, traders can act to earn excess profits on the basis of other information. The perfect markets theory or the efficient markets hypothesis (EMH) developed by Fama (1970, 1976), asserts that asset prices do in fact

36

reflect all available information. Thus in forming expectations about next period's price or rate of return, the market uses the correct probability distribution of stock returns and all available information. A difficulty encountered in testing Fama's hypothesis is that of specifying the behavior of expected returns or expected prices. In cases where empirical evidence results in rejecting stock market efficiency, the difficulty is not knowing whether it is the EMH or the model for expected returns that has been rejected.[11] Peel, Pope and Yadav (1993) note that changes in expectations regarding future dividends, interest rates and perceived risk premia affect stock prices, and since expectations are conditional upon available information, new information about relevant variables may affect price volatility. Volatility can increase if the frequency of information arrival increases. In this case, Edwards (1988) remarks that increased volatility may be a manifestation of a well functioning market. However, Edwards cautions that stock price volatility greater than that justified by objective new information makes prices inefficient by definition. The numerous studies on market efficiency in the finance literature can be interpreted as empirical studies of the informational efficiency of financial markets, and they represent tests of the implications of Fama's definition for market efficiency.

A related question that has received much attention in recent stock market research is whether volatility shocks themselves exhibit persistence over time, in other words, whether an interval of unusually high variance in returns is typically followed by high variance. It is important to know how long shocks to conditional variance last. For example, an increase in the conditional variance of stock market returns will typically cause the market risk premium to rise. If, however, the increase is short-lived, the term structure of the market risk premia may move only at the short end, and the valuation of long-lived assets may be affected only slightly (Poterba and Summers, 1986). No significant change to the risk premium will thus be made by the market and hence no significant changes in the discount factor or the price of a stock as determined by the net present value of the future expected cash flow will occur.

In the literature, mixed empirical results emerge regarding the duration of persistence together with the important economic implications of the volatility persistence issue. For example, Poterba and Summers (1986) argue that shocks to the US stock market are only short-lived, with a half-life of less than six months. They therefore reject Malkiel's (1979) and Pindyck's (1984) hypotheses that shocks to the investment environment during the early seventies were the most important factor explaining the market plunge during the mid-seventies. Chou (1988), however, reports a very different result. He finds the average half-life for volatility shocks have been about one year, which would cause the risk premium and consequently the price of stocks to change. A markedly low persistence is reported after the October 1987 crash, Schwert (1990a) finds that stock volatility returned to the pre-crash levels by early 1988. This short-lived property due to a stock market crash is not, however, observed for the smaller market downturns prior to 1987. It is noteworthy that Friedman and Laibson (1989), on modifying the ARCH model (examined in Chapter two) such that outliers, or extremely large shocks are allowed to have different dynamic effects than *ordinary* shocks, find that *ordinary* shocks tend to persist longer than outliers. In this case, ARCH models which fail to distinguish outliers from ordinary shocks tend to underestimate the persistence of *ordinary* shocks.

In summary, while we know that stock market volatility changes over time, that volatility tends to cluster, and volatility peaks are associated with price declines, we still know little about the fundamental causes of volatility in financial markets. While theory predicts that stock price changes should reflect changes in economic fundamentals, empirically the relationship is weak. Large stock price changes are often unrelated to identifiable economic developments, and stock price changes are often so volatile that they cannot be accounted for by measurable financial and economic factors. Evidence does suggest that time-varying behaviour and persistence of stock market volatility have been attributed to the uneven but persistent flow of information (e.g., Lamoureux and Lastrapes (1990); Gallant et al (1990)) and to changes in nominal interest rates and dividend yields (e.g., Campbell (1987); Attanasio and Wadhwani (1989)), to changes in the money supply (Engle and Rodrigues (1989)), and in margin requirements (Hardouvelis (1990)). Finally, Koutmos et al (1994) find that small capitalization markets (Australia, Belgium, Canada and Switzerland) exhibit considerably higher (three to five times larger) volatility persistence than large capitalization markets.

In conclusion, an important reason for our lack of knowledge regarding the causes of volatility is perhaps due to the lack of a direct theory which predicts how volatility will behave. Such a theory is unlikely to develop until the true price-setting process is known, but this in the end may never be known. Meanwhile, empirical tests and examination of volatility are the only alternative. The compilation and analysis of empirical results are likely to shed some light on these issues. An area of future research concerns the international evidence. The vast majority of published papers have investigated the volatility of the US stock markets, with, until recently, very few investigating the volatility of other stock markets. Chapter four of this book contributes to this literature by examining the causes of stock market volatility in Australia. Another area of research prompted by Shiller (1989) urges researchers to venture into the world of behavioural and psychological science to explain investor behaviour. Research in this area is young, data is difficult to find and results may be unlikely to be robust.

Speculative Bubbles and Noise

The possibility that asset prices might deviate from intrinsic values based on market fundamentals because of speculative bubbles or fads has long intrigued economists and financial analysts. This area of research has grown in its sophistication, volume and controversy. Camerer (1989) distinguishes three reasons why prices might deviate: rational growing bubbles, fads and information bubbles. The theory of rational bubbles is an example of a model in which expectations are formed rationally and the market is informationally efficient, but there are large deviations between market prices and fundamental values. Camerer notes that empirical tests appear to have little power to distinguish between growing rational bubbles and long-lived irrational fads. Prices deviate from intrinsic values because of fads, caused by socially-determined swings in utility from owning assets or in beliefs about intrinsic values. Information bubbles occur when temporary price swings occur during financial market trading hours. Information bubbles are caused by traders over-reacting or making imperfect inferences from the observed trading of others.

Galeotti and Schiantarelli (1994) investigate the relationship between fundamental and fad components of changes in stock prices and investment decisions by firms. Although the connection between the stock market and investment has been formalised in the context of the Q models of investment, empirical evidence on this connection is mixed. At the theoretical level, it is unclear whether firms should respond only to fundamentals or whether all share price movements including those caused by fad components of changes in stock prices should matter. To explain this phenomenon, Galeotti and Schiantarelli partition the change in the market value of shares into a fundamental and non-fundamental component, and assess their relationship with investment. Their results suggest that real investment appears to be significantly associated with movements in stock prices generated by fads. Irrational waves of optimism or pessimism in the mood of investors have therefore an important effect on firms' real decisions. The secondary question examined was whether changes in fundamentals matter more or less than fads in decisions regarding investment. The results indicate that changes in fundamentals have a greater effect on investment. However, this result is always insignificant in the case of new equity financing, while this is not true in the case of financing from retained earnings.

Financial Instability and Macroeconomic Activity

Kindleberger (1978) examined the association between financial crises, including sharp declines in stock prices, with subsequent declines in macroeconomic activity. The October 1929 crash and the depression of the 1930s represents an important case in point. A theory of business fluctuations that assigns a central role to stock market crashes in bringing about economic downturns must address two questions. *Firstly*, why would a decline in stock prices lead to a decline in real economic activity? *Secondly*, what causes the stock market itself to crash? On the first question, standard economic theory has had a fair amount to say, beginning with wealth effects on consumer spending and cost-of-capital effects on business investment, continuing through credit rationing effects due to loss of collateral value, and the effects of breakdown in one or more parts of the market mechanism, e.g. the collapse of the banking system. However, standard economic theory has had little to say about what causes the market to crash in the first place, with the exception of the 'financial instability hypothesis' advanced by Minsky (1977). The main point of Minsky's 'financial instability hypothesis' is that as the most recent crisis becomes a distant memory, relevant agents in the economy change their behaviour so as to erode the financial system's ability to withstand a major shock without sustaining a rupture of the kind typically associated with a severe downturn in real output and spending. In Minsky's description, the phenomenon mainly responsible for the deterioration over time of the economy's ability to withstand an adverse shock is the increasing prevalence of 'speculative' and even 'Ponzi' finance, in preference to 'hedge' finance.

In Minsky's terminology, a '*hedge*' financial structure[12] is one where the expected 'cash flows in' exceed the 'cash payment commitments' on the account of both principal and interest as far ahead as a reasonable person looks. In '*speculative*' or rollover financing, the net income portion of gross cash flow exceeds the interest payments committed, but the cash flows are insufficient to meet the payments commitments on principal. '*Ponz*' finance takes place when cash flows are not sufficient to pay the interest due on debt and the interest is folded into the principal owed. Given a shock that causes cash flows to be insufficient to service debt, this leads overextended borrowers to sell assets to meet obligations. An example of this is when the new liability structure for holding capital assets puts pressure on firms that are in '*speculative*' or '*Ponzi*' financing postures to use their cash flows to clean up their balance sheets, to use retained earnings to retire debt rather than as a basis for leveraged investment. Such making of positions by selling assets can well lead to a fall in the price of assets being offered. This will result in a smaller amount of cash being generated than the books indicate. This can lead to a broad erosion of firms' net worth and to a decline in the ability to finance investment. As a result investment falls and so does aggregate business profits. As Minsky has put it, 'selling positions in order to make positions' contributes to the decline in asset values. What prevents the economy from sustaining a rupture of the kind typically associated with a severe downturn in real output and spending? Minsky believes that, in today's world, large governments effectively prevent a collapse of profits, and central banks intervene to assure that during situations of potential crises not only banks but also other units that may otherwise be forced to make positions by trying to sell positions are refinanced. These two sets of intervention have successfully contained the aggregate reactions to the sometimes serious financial crises of the past decade.

The central phenomenon hypothesised by Minsky (1977) depends on the passage of time. As the perceived crash probability declines, the resulting true probability of a crash is actually rising. Lower probability of a crash leads

40

investors to take on increasingly extended and exposed positions, so the system as a whole becomes increasingly susceptible to a financial crisis in the event of an adverse shock. There is a contradiction here in that investors acting on the basis of a crash probability estimated from observed prior returns do not recognises the increased fragility of the system. On this apparent paradox, Minsky (1977) notes that the interval over which debt is built up is long enough for substantial changes in institutions to have occurred. Claims that more is known now than earlier and that policy is wiser now than in the past gain credence and affect expectations about system performance. Expectations formation takes into account that 'the world has changed' and that 'they won't let it happen', even though agents are not sure who 'they' are and what 'they' will do.

Friedman and Laibson (1989) link their empirical work to Minsky's 'financial instability hypothesis' by illustrating a model which conceptualises risk as consisting of an *ordinary* and *extraordinary* component. Their model attempts to explain empirically the kind of behaviour hypothesised by Minsky in characterising the irregular occurrence of financial crises with major negative effects on nonfinancial activity. Their data, representing stock price movements in the US since World War II, show too many extreme price movements (i.e. stock returns are leptokurtic) to fit the normal distribution. These extreme price movements overwhelmingly consist of market crashes, not rallies, which they label as *extraordinary* movements. They incorporate the latter by allowing stocks to have a two component form (i.e. *ordinary* and occasionally *extraordinary* component); people recognising this over time will be more willing to hold stocks, and correspondingly less willing to hold 'safe' assets (e.g. treasury bills). Investors willingness to hold stocks can, at best, stand for a metaphor for the public's willingness more generally to speculate on other assets and assume an extended liability position.

In the Friedman and Laibson model, market participants believe that stock returns consist of both an *ordinary* component, distributed normally (mean μ, variance σ_ε^2) and realised in each period, and an *extraordinary* component, of magnitude ψ, and having a probability ρ of being realised. After each new observation of returns, they therefore estimate ψ and ρ using all available information. Using these parameter values to estimate the probability of a stock market crash occurring, a risk-averse investor chooses a portfolio for the coming year. Typically this will take a more exposed position when the probability of a crash occurring is lower than when the probability of a crash is higher. As time passes since the most recent market crash, investors tend to perceive the probability of a crash as smaller, and hence take ever more exposed positions. It is not difficult to translate this behaviour into a much broader context, including, for example, business ventures in which the prospects for success hinge on whether a market crash does or does not occur. In any case the risk-averse investor is more likely to enter into any given risky transaction as the perceived probability of a crash is lower.

41

In both Minsky's 'financial instability hypothesis' and the empirical linkage to it by Friedman and Laibson, the cause of financial instability is primarily determined by what may be described as the onset of a *financial crises* or the occurrence of an *extraordinary* movement in stock markets as has occurred periodically in capitalist economies. The linkages to the real economy, although occasionally implied, are not explicit in terms of the effects increased financial volatility may have on real economic activity prior to the actual financial crises. In the following section we examine developing countries experiences who experimented with financial liberalisation, with the objective of analysing the effects financial liberalisation has had on real economic activity. Here we are not primarily concerned with an impending financial crises *per se* but with the implications for economic activity in those countries which experimented with financial liberalisation programmes.

Financial Volatility and Financial Liberalization in Developing Countries

Grabel (1995a) argues that financial liberalization leads to 'speculation-led economic development', which is characterised by a preponderance of risky investment practices and shaky financial structures. Furthermore, financial liberalization is likely to induce an increase in unproductive profit-seeking activities, a greater likelihood of financial crises, a misallocation of credit and ultimately, diminished rates of real sector economic growth. Grabel's (1995a) explanation for the experiences of developing countries who experimented with financial liberalization programmes identifies three main components affecting demand and supply. The demand-side effects are listed here and briefly explained below. *High interest rates* discourage all but high risk and high expected return investment projects. This results is the creation of an *adverse* pool of projects, characterised by various forms of speculative activities such as leveraged buyouts of industrial enterprises and generally what Minsky (1986) refers to as '*Ponzi*' finance schemes. *Institutional innovations and speculation* allow financial instruments to give investors the apparent protection of instantaneous withdrawal of funds by transforming illiquid real sector investments in plant and equipment into financial claims that can trade hands as quickly as the institutional and technological structures permit. Grabel notes the ability to 'churn' assets in this way provides a degree of apparent security to the financial investor that is not available to the industrial corporation which has undertaken long-term capital investment. His claim, however, that the relative independence of financial asset values from underlying 'fundamentals' imparts an extreme variability to these asset values is not substantiated. *Increasing interest rate spread* is a consequence of the increasing volatility of asset prices and the concomitant decline in the security of collateral. The increase in speculative activity relative to total economic activity, ensues that banks will be expected to exact a higher risk premium in the form of higher interest rates, especially so in the case of long-term debt. This pattern of financing only increases the susceptibility of real-sector investment to interest rate shocks, as the continuance of the project comes to depend on favorable short-term rates. Supply-side changes combine to compel lenders to validate and encourage the adverse class of investment projects likely to flourish following financial liberation.

Other studies have provided similar accounts of developing countries' experience with financial liberalisation including DeLong et al, (1989) and Snowden (1987) who give several examples of upward pressure on interest rates in order to justify the increase in risk associated with high risk high return type investments. DeLong makes the point that there is an increased likelihood that the economy becomes more susceptible to financial crises with disruptive slipover effects in the real sector. Wolfson (1986 and 1990) shows that a variety of surprise macroeconomic events (for example, a sudden rise in interest rates) can ultimately threaten a fragile financial structure, leading to loan defaults. Banks fearing a collapse in profitability may cut back on lending, commencing a credit crunch with a decline in aggregate economic activity.[13]

A catalyst for analysing developing economies' experience with financial liberalisation has no doubt been the enormous growth in stock market activity of these countries. For example in 1980 the stock markets listed domestic companies in developing countries had a market capitalisation of $86,000 US million and a trading volume of $23,000 million. By the end of 1992, these same countries domestic companies had a combined capitalisation of $774,000 million and an annual trading volume of $594,000 million. Grabel (1995b) makes the point that the degree to which expanded stock markets are an impediment to real sector growth and stability in developing countries, depends in part on the level of volatility they exhibit, 'markets with frequent and severe swings might be much more apt to induce short-term speculative investment practices . . . and be more likely to induce speculative activity . . . (and) induce broader macroeconomic instability' (p. 904).

Grabel acknowledges, however, the importance of measuring volatility as a first step towards an empirical assessment of the effects of stock market volatility in developing economies. The indices she develops to measure volatility in these markets are flawed in several respects (see below). Based on the limited data available to her, Grabel concludes that financial liberalisation induces increased asset price volatility which is corroborated in the majority of countries investigated. Grabel constructs two volatility indices (VIs). The first of these she refers to as *the neo-classical* index (NC-VI); here assets yield some 'normal' return over time based on their underlying fundamental values. The magnitude of the deviation from the assets fundamentals-based return constitutes asset volatility. In the NC-VI version, the realised return on an asset in any period t (R_t) is equal to the sum of its expected return for that period (E_t) and the innovation in returns (I_t) thus; $R_t = E_t|_{t-1} + I_t$ where $E(I_t) = 0$ and $E(I_t^2) = \sigma2$. In this measure the innovation term is assumed to have standard statistical properties (randomly distributed with zero mean and constant variance). However this representation fails to present a true picture of the asset return series stochastic properties necessary for properly modeling these dependencies. In particular these measures fail to catch time varying behavior and persistence of stock market volatility. Similar problems relate to Grabel's *Keynesian* volatility index, here asset returns have no *'fundamentals-based centre of gravity'* volatility is simply given by the magnitude of asset return fluctuations. The Keynesian measure of market volatility over some interval is simply the coefficient of variation defined as KVI = σ/mean price. Despite the inherent problems with Grabel's measures failing to correct for autocorrelation and heteroskedasticity in the return series, Grabel's results corroborates anecdotal evidence of increased financial volatility following financial liberalisation in developing countries.

Monetary Volatility

The theoretical rationale advanced for studying the macroeconomic effects of money growth is that money growth variability increases the variability of interest rates which in turn increases the risk of holding bonds. Increased risk of holding bonds raises money demand, hence the general level of interest rates rise, and investment and output fall. Several studies by, *inter alia*, Mascaro and Meltzer (1983), Belongia (1984), Tatom (1985) and McMillin (1988), all relating to the US economy, find evidence of a significant linkage from either monetary or interest rate volatility to the level of real economic activity, although Evans (1984) finds evidence only from interest rate volatility rather than from monetary volatility. The most general of these studies by McMillan (1988) allows both monetary and interest rate volatility to influence a set of macroeconomic variables, and reports that monetary growth volatility has strong effects on interest rates, the level of real output and prices. Al-Saji (1992) provides strong support for the hypothesis that rising money growth and interest rate volatility affect real variables, such as output and employment for Italy and the UK, while Al-Saji (1994) demonstrates that both money growth volatility and interest rate volatility exert a significant and negative effect on the level of real output.

Evans (1984) uses a methodology developed by Barro (1978, 1981), to try to find out whether money growth and interest rate volatility affect the level of output for the US economy over the period 1947-1981. Evans finds that the stagnation of the US economy since 1979 stemmed almost as much from increased interest rate volatility as from reduced money growth. He finds that the Federal Reserve policy of disinflation in October 1979 led to an unanticipated increase in interest rate volatility which reduced output by about 1 percent in 1980 and by about 2.5 percent in 1981 and 1982. Under the new policy, the Federal Reserve would try to hit its monetary targets in the short run, while allowing interest rates to become much more volatile. Mascaro and Meltzer

(1983) also argue that the Federal Reserve policy of moving away from pegging the federal funds rate within narrow bands, to focusing its attention on controlling money growth created higher interest rate volatility along with increased money growth volatility which raised real interest rates and depressed the economy. Evans believes like many nonmonetarists that increased interest rate volatility has disrupted financial markets, increased the risk that agents face in these markets, and may have depressed the economy unnecessarily.

Theoretical Considerations

Monetary theory would appear to provide several answers to questions regarding the transmission mechanism by which monetary changes spill over into the real sector, namely asset, product and factor markets. However, a consensus on what it is exactly the transmission mechanism is supposed to affect, and on the direction of causation has still to be accepted amongst economists. Hicks (1967, pp. 156) believed that 'Monetary theory (to be) less abstract than most economic theory: it cannot avoid a relation to reality, which in other economic theory is sometimes missing'. By less abstract, Hicks of course does not necessarily imply that monetary theory is any less complex.

Monetarists regard the transmission mechanism first proposed by Irving Fisher (1923) as the basis for their book. This equation states that MV = PT, where the right hand side of the equation corresponds to the transfer of goods, services, or securities with the left-hand side, corresponding to the matching transfer of money. The right-hand side is regarded as the aggregate of payments during some interval, with P a suitable chosen average of the prices and T a suitable chosen aggregate of the quantities during that interval. PT represents a flow of physical goods and services over an interval of time. The left-hand side of the equation treats money as a stock. For a single transaction, where cash is turned over once, V = 1, M is measured in dollars, so the product MV is dollars per unit time.

A frequent criticism of the quantity theory concerns the mechanism whereby a change in the nominal quantity of money is transmitted to prices and quantities. The criticism is that the transmission mechanism is not specified, that the proponents of the quantity theory rely on a black box connecting the input (i.e. the nominal quantity of money) and the output (i.e. the effects on prices and quantities). In an attempt to answer this criticism, Friedman and Schwartz (1963) examined the relationship between the variability of money and income (nominal) for both the US and the UK, and found that over the post World War II period, the variability of money to be greater relative to that of income.[14] Friedman and Schwartz concluded that over long periods, differential rates of monetary growth are reflected primarily in differential rates of inflation and have little effect on output, whereas over brief periods, differential rates of monetary growth affect both prices and output. These results are confirmed by Friedman and Schwartz (1982) for the US but not for the UK. Generally, they find that a permanent one percentage point increase in the rate

45

of monetary growth will ultimately be reflected in a one percentage point increase in the rates of growth of both nominal income and prices, leaving the rate of growth of output unchanged. In their view money illusion is a transitory phenomenon, if it occurs at all.

Friedman and Schwartz (1982) argue that deviations of nominal income from its anticipated growth path, produced by deviations of monetary growth from its anticipated path, will produce deviations in output from the path that would be mandated by real factors alone.[15] Unanticipated changes in nominal income alter the demand for particular products. Output is affected (in the short run) because sellers and producers of these products have no way (at the outset) of knowing whether the change in demand for their products is a change relative to the demand for other products, to which it is in their interest to react by expanding or contracting output, or a change in general nominal demand, to which the appropriate response is an adjustment of prices. The central idea in the monetarists book is that changes in the money supply explain changes in money income, real output (in the short run only), and the price level in the long run.

Exogenous Versus Endogenous Money

In the orthodox view, the monetary authorities control the money supply (e.g. M1 and M3) via control over the amount of bank reserves, giving rise to the following formula: $M = m.B$, where M is the money stock, m is the money multiplier and B is base money defined as the bank reserves plus currency held by the non-bank public. The direction of causation runs from B to M; an exogenous money assumes that central bank actions determine its size.

In the classical world, money is neutral. It can only affect nominal not real values. Monetarists believe that the economy is basically stable, and only exogenous events such as wars, droughts, strikes, shifts in expectations, and changes in foreign demand may cause variations in output around the trend path. Over the short run, monetarists believe that the major source of economic instability is the mismanagement of the money supply by the monetary authorities. While monetarists believe that the monetary authorities control the money supply, they reject using the money supply as a countercyclical measure. The reason for this is due to the presence of time lags which are of an unpredictable length, such that the time interval between changes in money stock and the affect of this change on other variables is completely unknown.[16]

According to Keynes (1963), money plays a role of its own. It is not neutral. Money, as Keynes said, '... affects motives and decisions and is, in short, one of the operative factors in the situation, so that the course of events cannot be predicted, either in the long period or in the short, without a knowledge of the behaviour of money between the first state and the last. And this is what we ought to mean when we speak of a Monetary Economy'.[17] Keynes believed that the relationship between money and the economic activity is linked by the level of investment and the rate of interest is determined by people's holding of a portfolio of assets, consisting of money and bonds. Where government wants to vary the money supply, it would have to induce people to exchange bonds for money. Changes in money supply affected the interest rate and thus real activity via investment.

In the post-Keynesian and institutionalist framework, money is regarded as endogenous. Arestis (1988) and Arestis and Eichner (1988) provide the main elements of what constitutes post-Keynesian monetary theory. Essentially 'Money is viewed as the outcome of credit creation; it is a residual and as such it cannot be the cause of changes in any economic magnitudes' (Arestis, 1988. pp. 66) and 'A system of payments based on checks makes it possible, though the process by which banks makes loans, to vary the amount of funds in circulation in response to changes in the level of real economic activity' Arestis and Eichner (1988b, pp. 1005). Within the post-Keynesian and institutionalist analysis the direction of causation is completely reversed compared to the analysis where money is viewed as exogenous and should read B = (1/m)M where the causation is from M to B. According to Arestis and Eichner (1988b, pp.1007) in the UK 'monetary authorities have consistently followed an accommodating policy, providing banks with reserves they need to meet the credit needs of their customers ... For the monetary authorities to act in any other manner would, in fact, be contrary to the purpose for which central banks have been established . . . to act as lender of last resort and preserve liquidity of the banking system'.[18] Moore (1988) observes that while Post-Keynesians argue that the growth of money wages is more exogenous, compared to money, central banks are forced to accommodate money wage increases to prevent unemployment rates from rising to politically unacceptable levels. Moore also points out that until the Post-Keynesians are able to specify more closely the mechanism by which changes in money wages influence money stock, they are like the monetarists open to the accusation of having a 'Black Box'.

In summary, the role of money in business cycle fluctuations is still a controversial issue. Keynesians and monetarists (in the short-run only) hold the view that money affects economic activity. By contrast, Post-Keynesians believe that money does not affect real economic activity, the direction of causation being from economic activity to money. The role of money in the Post-Keynesian world is to solely accommodate the demands for money and credit from bank's customers. The implication of this is that money supply can accommodate itself to changes in the level of GNP (Post-Keynesian) or from a Keynesian perspective that money can influence GNP via the level of investment. From an Australian perspective a review of the practice of Monetary Policy over the past 20 years may provide further insights on the issue from the perspective of a small open economy.

Monetary Policy in Australia: Empirical Evidence

A frequently asked question, bearing in mind the above discussion, is which variable should be used as an indicator of monetary policy? There are several to choose from: the growth rate of the money supply; the nominal interest rate; the real interest rate; and the yield curve. Milbourne (1995) reviews the performance of each indicator, and finds that each indicator has specific problems when it comes to tracking the performance of monetary policy. Money supply (M3) has been used as a guide to policy in Australia from about 1977 until 1985. Over the last decade the growth rate of M3 has been erratic and largely unrelated to other variables in the economy. Nominal interest rates have also been used as an indicator of policy. In times of high inflation (as in Australia over the late 80s and early 90s), the nominal interest rate is not the appropriate interest rate facing investors or borrowers. The yield curve compares the difference between long and short-term interest rates. Empirical evidence on each of these transmission mechanisms is mixed. The evidence before 1977 and after 1984 shows reasonably good correlation between M3 and real income growth (gross national expenditure, GNE), but not during the intervening period of monetary targeting via M3. Does monetary policy affect economic activity via interest rates? Milbourne used simple time series plots of the growth rate of private investment against real (ex-post) interest rates without finding any evident correlation between the two. Equally, the new Keynesian argument that there should be a direct relationship between credit and income found little support within Australia. Plotting the growth in business investment (real) and business credit, as well as private expenditure (real) and personal credit, displays no better correlation than that between money and output. In this respect Milbourne notes that Keynesian theories are no better than the orthodox transmission mechanism.

Since financial deregulation commenced with the floating of the Australian dollar in December 1983, the Reserve Bank has used interest rates as their main instrument of monetary policy. To tighten monetary policy, the Reserve Bank sells securities to financial institutions via authorised money market dealers. The dealers finance their purchases by bidding for funds from other financial institutions. This leads to an increase in cash rates, and subsequently in all other interest rates. Thus monetary policy can exert influence over short-term interest rates and affect the real economy through interest sensitive components of aggregate demand. Has financial deregulation changed the mechanism by which monetary policy affects the real economy? One possibility is that since monetary policy now effects the entire financial system rather than just banks, its effects on the real economy are enhanced.

Australia's conduct of monetary policy via monetary targets (in particular M3) was abandoned in January 1985. This was replaced by an approach which uses all major economic and financial factors, present and prospective. These include the state of the economy, the balance of payments, prices, monetary factors namely interest rates, the exchange rate and monetary aggregates. These are viewed regularly and an 'on balance' judgment is made about monetary policy. Critiques of the *check list* approach say that monetary policy as conducted in Australia is highly volatile, and certainly more volatile than monetary policy in the major OECD countries. Morgan (1990) suggests that this volatility can be traced back to the ambiguity flowing from the check list approach. Since the check list approach is a mismatch of ultimate targets, intermediate targets and instruments, the ultimate objective of monetary policy can become clouded. Since 1990 the RBA has officially declared that the maintenance of the current low rate of inflation as the prime target of the medium-term, and for stabilisation policy to respond only to major fluctuations in the economy rather than fine tuning.

Policy and Financial Asset Price Volatility

While the evidence on financial asset price volatility covered in the literature is voluminous and improves our understanding of the nature of volatility, the vast majority of these studies ignores the impact of policy as a possible economic explanation for financial asset price volatility.[19] In an attempt to remedy this deficiency in the literature on financial volatility and its relationship to real economic activity, this book performs an empirical investigation into aspects of the connection between policy and financial volatility.

In order to identify whether policy contributes to financial asset price volatility, two chapters in this book investigate the connection between monetary and fiscal policy and the volatility of financial assets and other macroeconomic variables. In particular, Chapter five examines the relationship between monetary growth and real output volatility, Chapter six investigates the relationship between fiscal financing innovations and exchange rate variability, and Chapter seven provides empirical evidence on the relationship between exchange rate volatility and trade flows within a multi-country empirical model.

Summary and Conclusions

In the discussion of the real business cycle paradigm, financial factors are completely absent since the Modligliani-Miller theorem applies, hence financial structure is both irrelevant and indeterminate. Consequently, this paradigm offers us no explanation for economic depressions where breakdown in financial trade plays a major role, while the paradigm is also silent about regular movements of financial variables. Evidence from finance studies indicates that financial asset prices have shown significant changes in volatility over recent times. Finance theory based on the efficient markets hypothesis rests on the assumption that market prices incorporate all public information about fundamentals. However, the evidence suggests significant deviations of stock prices from market fundamentals, this evidence coming predominantly from the US. Furthermore it was noted that significant increases in stock market volatility have been experienced from time to time. A range of factors appear responsible with persistence of stock market volatility high on the list. A firm's financial structure as explained by Minsky's financial instability hypothesis provides us with an explanation for major financial breakdown but little explanation of the consequence of increased stock market volatility for real economic activity. Monetary theory would appear to provide several answers to questions regarding the transmission mechanism by which monetary changes spill over into the real sector, namely asset, product and factor markets.

However, a consensus on what exactly the transmission mechanism is, and on the direction of causation, is an issue yet to be resolved amongst economists. Empirical evidence on the performance of monetary policy appears to be dogged by the poor performance of monetary policy indicators. Finally, given that financial economics appears to provide little by way of an economic explanation for volatility, this book attempts to identify whether policy contributes to financial asset price volatility. In particular, it investigates the connection between the execution of monetary and fiscal policy and the volatility of financial assets and other macroeconomic variables. Before moving to this we will first carry out an empirical investigation into the causes of stock market volatility. This is done in the next chapter.

4 The Causes of Stock Market Volatility in Australia

Introduction

The issue of stock market volatility has received much attention in the finance literature. The main issues which have been addressed include, the important causes of stock market volatility, and whether it increased over time, the extent to which international financial integration led to a faster transmission of volatility across international stock markets, and the role, if any, regulators ought to play in the process. Previous researchers have examined these issues. On the causes of stock market volatility, Officer (1973) examines the effects of volatility in business cycle variables, Black (1976) and Christie (1982) relate stock market volatility to financial leverage, Merton (1980), Poterba and Summers (1986) and French, Schwert and Staumbaugh (1987) relate stock market volatility to the volatility of expected returns, and Schwert (1989) conducts an extensive array of tests on the macroeconomic causes of stock market volatility over long runs of monthly data for the US. The issue of whether the world's financial and capital markets are now transmitting volatility more quickly has been examined by Koch and Koch (1991), Malliaris and Urrutia (1992), Chan, Karolyi and Stulz (1992) and Rahman and Yung (1994). The related issue of whether stock market volatility has increased over time has been investigated by Peel, Pope and Yadav (1993), while Scott (1991) and Timmermann (1993) examine the extent to which the volatility of stock prices determines their underlying value.

The purpose of this chapter is to contribute to the literature on the causes of stock market volatility by examining the determinants of movements in the volatility of equity returns in a small, internationally integrated stock market. The Australian stock market serves as an especially illuminating example in this regard insofar as it is increasingly integrated with the important international stock markets throughout Asia and the rest of the world. Previous research on the volatility of the Australian stock market includes the work of Brailsford and Faff (1993) and Kearns and Pagan (1993), both of whom examined the relative explanatory power of alternative models of conditional volatility, but neither of whom related stock market volatility to the volatility of financial and business cycle variables. This chapter develops and estimates a model which is capable of explaining the financial and business cycle determinants of movements in the conditional volatility of the Australian All Industrials stock market index.

The results presented in this chapter constitute new evidence which is interpretable as an extension of the low frequency analysis of Schwert (1989) who did not include international factors such as the current account deficit and the exchange rate in his investigation of the causes of stock market volatility in the US. In addition, Schwert's (1989) vector autoregressive model of the determination of conditional stock market volatility, along with other research which employs the same methodology, suffers from the generated regressors problem (see *inter alia*, Pagan (1984, 1986); McAleer and McKenzie (1991); and Oxley and McAleer (1993)) which yields inefficient estimates, introduces bias into a number of diagnostic test statistics and generates potentially invalid inferences. This problem is overcome in the current chapter by jointly estimating the equation for the conditional volatility of the Australian stock market index together with the equations determining the conditional volatilities of all variables included in the model using the Generalised Least Squares (GLS) estimation procedure and the Hendry general-to-specific estimation strategy. Related research by Koutoulas and Kryzanowski (1996) employs a similar methodology to that which is employed in this chapter in order to examine the explanatory power of macroeconomic conditional volatilities in an arbitrage pricing model of monthly Canadian stock market returns. Interestingly, they find that the conditional volatilities of industrial production and the exchange rate feature in their model, while the conditional volatility of interest rates play a more ambiguous role.

The chapter is structured as follows. The next Section describes the theoretical framework which motivates the empirical analysis and describes the dataset which is used for the study. Following this we focus our attention on the causes of volatility in the Australian stock market. Specifically, we employ a Generalised Least Squares (GLS) estimation methodology to implement the Davidian and Carroll (1987) ARCH model of conditional volatility to model the determination of the Australian stock market conditional volatility using the Hendry general-to-specific estimation methodology (see Mizon (1995) for a recent overview). The final Section reviews the main results and draws together the conclusions.

Theory, Methodology and Data

The price of equity at any point in time is equal to the discounted present value of expected future cash flows (including capital gains and dividends) to shareholders:

$$E_t S_t^i = E_t \sum_{k=1}^{\infty} \frac{D_{t+k}^i}{(1+r_{t+k}^i)^k} \qquad (4.1)$$

where Q_t^i is the price of asset i, C^i, denotes the cash flows associated with it, R denotes the interest rate and E_{t-1} is the expectations operator. In an open economic and financial system such as that which prevails in Australia, corporate cash flows, C^i, are influenced by developments in the macroeconomy such as the level of aggregate industrial production (IP), the money supply (M) and the level of prices (P), the external trading position of the country as measured by the current account deficit of the balance of payments (D) and the spot exchange rate (S) which is defined as the domestic currency price of foreign exchange.

In moving from equity prices to returns, let q_t^i denote the actual return on asset i, and let $\hat{q}_t^i = E_t\left[q_t^i / I_{t-1}\right]$ denote its expected return conditional on the available information set at time t-1. In addition, let $\sigma_t^{q^i}$ denote the unconditional standard deviation of returns on asset i, and let $\hat{\sigma}_t^{q^i} = E_t[\sigma_t^{q^i} / I_{t-1}]$ denote its conditional counterpart. From equation (4.1), the conditionally expected return on asset i is a function, f, of the conditionally expected determinants of the discounted cash flows,

$$E_t\left[q_t^i / I_{t-1}\right] = f\{E_t[C_t^i(IP_t M_t, P_t, D_t, S_t), R_t] / I_{t-1}\} \qquad (4.2)$$

and the conditional standard deviation of returns is a function, g, of the conditional standard deviations of the determinants of the cash flows.

$$E_t[\sigma_t^{q^i} / I_{t-1}] = g\{E_t[\sigma_t^{IP}, \sigma_t^M, \sigma_t^P, \sigma_t^D, \sigma_t^S, \sigma_t^R] / I_{t-1}\} \qquad (4.3)$$

In order to empirically implement the model, we must obtain monthly estimates of the standard deviations of the relevant variables. Although this can be achieved with ease for the stock market and financial variables such as interest rates and exchange rates, business cycle data are not typically available at higher frequencies than monthly. Accordingly, the approach adopted here is to employ the methodology of Davidian and Carroll (1987). Let X denote the vector of stock market and business cycle variables employed in the study, ie., $X = X (Q,$ $IP, M, P, D, S, R)$, let σ_t^x denote the unconditional standard deviation of these variables, and let $\hat{\sigma}_t^x = E_t(\sigma_t^x / I_{t-1})$ denote the corresponding conditional standard deviations. The latter are obtained as $\hat{\sigma}_t^x = \sigma_t^x - \varepsilon_{2,t}^x$ from the following regression:

53

$$\sigma_t^x = \beta_1(H)\sigma_t^x + \sum_{m=1}^{12} \beta_m SD_{m,t} + \varepsilon_{2,t}^x \qquad (4.4)$$

where $\beta_1(H)$ is a 12th order polynomial in the lag operator H, the SD_m 's are monthly dummy variables to capture seasonal variations in the means and standard deviations of the variables, and the σ_t^x are innovations which are obtained as the absolute values of the residuals from the following equation, ie., $\sigma_t^x = /\varepsilon_{1,t}^x /$ where,

$$\varepsilon_{1,t}^x = \Delta Log(X)_t - E_t(\Delta Log(X)_t / I_{t-1})$$

$$= \Delta Log(X)_t - \alpha_1(H)\Delta Log(X)_t - \sum_{m=1}^{12} \alpha_m SD_{m,t} \qquad (4.5)$$

and $\alpha_1(H)$ is another 12th order polynomial in the lag operator H. The measure of conditional volatility in equation (4.4) represents a generalisation of the 12-month rolling standard estimator used by Officer (1973), Fama (1976) and Merton (1980) to measure stock market volatility, because it allows the conditional mean to vary over time in equation (4.5) while also allowing different weights to apply to the lagged absolute unpredicted changes in stock market returns in equation (4.4). This measure has been used by Schwert (1989) to examine the relationship between stock market volatility and underlying economic volatility, and more recently by Koutoulas and Kryzanowski (1996) to examine the role of conditional macroeconomic factors in an arbitrage pricing model. The relative merits of alternative measures of conditional volatility are reviewed by, *inter alia*, Engle (1993) and Diebold and Lopez (1995), while Kearney (1996) elaborates on the measure employed here and points to the implications for financial regulatory policies. It is similar to the autoregressive conditional heteroscedasticity (ARCH) model of Engle (1982) which, in its various forms, has been widely used in the finance literature. Davidian and Carroll (1987) argue that the specification in equation (4.4) based on the absolute value of the prediction errors is more robust than those based on the squared residuals in equation (4.5).

The dataset for the study consists of monthly observations on the Australian stock market and business cycle variables including the interest rate on 3-month bank accepted bills, the Australian - US dollar exchange rate, the rate of inflation of the wholesale price index, the current account deficit and the level of industrial production over the period July 1970 - January 1994. Table 4.1 contains detailed descriptions of all variables used in the analysis together with their source.

Modeling the Conditional Volatility of the Australian Stock Market

In order to appropriately account for the non-zero cross equation covariances which arise from the generated regressors problem (see, *inter alia*, Pagan (1984, 1986); McAleer and McKenzie (1991); and Oxley and McAleer (1993)), the equation for the conditional volatility of the Australian stock market index is estimated jointly with the equations determining the conditional volatilities of all variables included in the model using the Generalised Least Squares (GLS) estimation procedure. The GLS estimator is described by first stacking the system to be estimated in the following form with M equations and T observations:

$$\begin{bmatrix} y_1 \\ \vdots \\ y_m \end{bmatrix} = \begin{bmatrix} X_1 & \cdots & 0 \\ & & \\ 0 & \cdots & X_m \end{bmatrix} \begin{bmatrix} \beta_1 \\ \vdots \\ \beta_m \end{bmatrix} + \begin{bmatrix} \varepsilon_1 \\ \vdots \\ \varepsilon_m \end{bmatrix} \tag{4.6}$$

where y is an $MT \times 1$ vector of dependent variables, X is an $MT \times (\sum_{i=1}^{M} K_i)$ matrix of explanatory variables, β is an $MT \times (\sum_{i=1}^{M} K_i)$ matrix of coefficients and ε is an $MT \times 1$ vector of errors. In the model analysed here, (4.6) contains 15 equations (ie., $M = 15$) with 259 observations (ie., $T = 259$) on each variable. The first seven equations are given by equation (4.5) for each variable in the X vector, the next seven equations are given by equation (4.4) for each variable in the X vector, and the last equation is given by:

$$\hat{\sigma}_t^Q = \lambda_0 + \lambda_1(K)\hat{\sigma}_t^x + \varepsilon_{3,t} \tag{4.7}$$

where the X vector is X *(Q, IP, M, P, D, S, R)* as before, and the $\lambda_1(K)$ are polynomials of the 4th degree in the lag operator, K. Equation (4.7) relates the conditional volatility of the Australian stock market, Q, to the conditional volatility of the Australian financial and business cycle variables including industrial production, *IP*, the money supply, *M*, inflation, *P*, the current account deficit, *D*, the exchange rate, *S*, and the interest rate, *R*.

   The system in equation (4.6) incorporates the possibility of cross-equation correlation amongst the error terms which yields the following covariance matrix of errors:

$$E(\varepsilon\varepsilon') = \Omega = \begin{bmatrix} \sigma_{11}I & ..... & \sigma_{1G}I \\ & & \\ \sigma_{G1}I & ..... & \sigma_{GG}I \end{bmatrix}.$$

Writing the system in matrix form as in equation (4.8), we can describe the GLS estimator as given by equation (4.9):

$$y = X\beta + \varepsilon \qquad (4.8)$$

$$\hat{\beta} = (X'\Omega^{-1}X)^{-1}X'\Omega^{-1}y. \qquad (4.9)$$

The gain in efficiency of this GLS estimator over OLS estimation depends on a number of factors including the extent of relation across the equations in the system and the extent to which the X variables differ across equations. In the current context of estimating the conditional volatilities of financial and economic variables, the potential for efficiency gain by estimating the system by GLS is considerable.

Table 4.2 presents the summary statistics from the OLS estimates of the first 12 autoregressions contained in equations (4.4) and (4.5) which are used as inputs during the GLS estimation procedure. Looking firstly at the top part of the Table which summarises the equations for the conditional means, the equations explain between 7 and 79 percent of the variation in the dependent variables, with, as expected, the financial variables (including the stock market returns, the interest rate and the exchange rate) occupying the lower end of the explanatory power rankings. The equations are all free from higher order autocorrelation as evidenced by the Ljung-Box Q-statistics. The sums of the lagged dependent coefficients (with their marginal significance levels in brackets) are presented in the fourth column of the Table under the heading of *Sum*. The columns headed by F_1 and F_2 provide the F-statistics for the joint exclusion of, respectively, all lagged dependents and all the seasonal variables in each regression. The lagged dependents in the equations for the stock market, inflation and the current account deficit are jointly significant in their respective equations, while the seasonal dummy variables are jointly significant in all equations except those for inflation and the exchange rate. With regard to the Australian stock market, the latter finding is in conformity with other researchers such as Gultekin and Gultekin (1983) who found statistically significant stock market seasonality in 14 out of 17 countries studied, Kramer (1994) who related stock market seasonality in the US to underlying macroeconomic seasonality, and Haugen and Jorian

(1996) who have reported that the January effect has not declined in size during the past three decades in the US.

Looking next at the bottom part of the Table which summarises the equations for the conditional standard deviations, the equations explain predictably less of the variation in the dependent variables, and all are free from higher order autocorrelation as evidenced by:

Table 4.1: Variables Used and Data Sources

Q: Australian sharemarket All Industrials Index, sampled on close of trading on the last trading day in the month. The index is re-based to 1973=100. Source is *Australian Stock Exchange*.

IP: The monthly percentage change in the index of industrial production, rebased to 1973=100. Source is OECD Economic Database.

P: The monthly index of wholesale prices in Australia, re-based to 1973=100. Source is OECD Economic Database.

I: The monthly percentage change in the wholesale price index (P) in Australia, re-based to 1975=100. Source is OECD Economic Database.

D: The current account deficit of the balance of payments in Australia, in billions of Australian dollars. Source is OECD Economic Database.

S: The spot exchange rate of the Australian - US dollar exchange rate, sampled at the end of the last trading day each month. Source is OECD Economic Database.

R: The interest rate on three-month bank accepted bills in Australia, sampled at the end of the last trading day each month. Source is Reserve Source Bank of Australia.

$CRASH$: Dummy variable to capture the effects of the October 1987 stock market crash. It takes the value of 1 in October 1987 and 0 at all other times.

SD: Monthly seasonal dummy variables to capture the effects of monthly variations the conditional mean and conditional standard deviations of the business cycle and financial variables.

Table 4.2: Estimation Results of the ARCH Models of Stock Market Returns and Business Cycle Variables, July 1970 - January 1994

Variable	R^2	SEE	Q	Sum	F_1	F_2

$$X_t = \sum_{j=1}^{12} \delta_j^x X_{t-j} - \sum_{m=1}^{12} \eta_m D_{m,t} + \xi_t^x$$

Variable	R^2	SEE	Q	Sum	F_1	F_2
Q	.21	.047	51.05 (.05)*	-3.81 (6.05)*	35.82 (.00)*	2.43 (.01)*
Y	.79	.062	24.20 (.93)	-0.90 (0.01)	1.75 (.06)	2.83 (.00)*
M	.62	.014	30.44 (.73)	0.33 (1.90)	1.72 (.06)	10.39 (.00)*
P	.22	.016	20.27 (.98)	0.42 (2.89)*	4.74 (.00)*	1.34 (.20)
D	.53	.123	38.27 (.37)	-1.94 (3.65)*	15.41 (.00)*	3.75 (.00)*
E	.07	.030	20.43 (.98)	-0.02 (0.10)	1.20 (.29)	0.47 (.93)
R	.21	.081	22.77 (.96)	0.31 (1.69)	1.74 (.06)	2.52 (.00)*

$$\sigma_t^x = \sum_{j=1}^{12} \alpha_j^x \sigma_{t-j}^x + \sum_{m=1}^{12} \beta_m D_{m,t} + \varepsilon_t^x$$

Variable	R^2	SEE	Q	Sum	F_1	F_2
Q	.20	.029	19.04 (.99)	0.49 (3.70)*	4.00 (.00)*	1.91 (.03)*
Y	.32	.039	21.37 (.97)	0.55 (4.82)*	6.20 (.00)*	3.35 (.00)*
M	.10	.009	25.85 (.89)	0.22 (1.10)	0.94 (.51)	2.54 (.00)*
P	.07	.011	29.92 (.75)	0.34 (2.15)*	1.02(.43)	1.74 (.06)
D	.15	.007	22.37 (.96)	0.42 (2.45)*	1.18 (.30)	2.64 (.00)*
E	.08	.023	26.81 (.87)	0.33 (1.87)	1.12 (.34)	1.68 (.07)
R	.17	.054	19.95 (.99)	0.62 (4.83)*	2.83 (.00)*	1.97 (.03)*

Note: The Table presents the regression summary results for equations (2) and (3) in the text, regressed on each variable in the Table. *SEE* denotes the standard error of the regression and Q denotes the Ljung-Box test for higher order autocorrelation. *Sum* denotes the sums of coefficients of the lagged dependent variables in each regression equation. F_1 denotes the F-statistics for the joint exclusion of all lagged dependents in each regression. F_2 denotes the F-statistics for the joint exclusion of all the seasonal coefficients in each regression. Marginal significance levels for these test statistics are presented in the brackets.

the Ljung-Box Q-statistics. The lagged dependents in the equations for the stock market, industrial production, inflation, the current account deficit and the interest rate are jointly significant in their respective equations, while the seasonal dummy variables are, as in the top part of the Table, jointly significant in the equations for all variables except inflation and the exchange rate.

Figure 4.1 presents time series plots of the conditional volatilities of all variables used in the study. Most series display considerable time variation in their volatilities. Of particular note is the high volatility of interest rates during the 1980s and the stock market volatility associated with the October 1987 crash. The summary statistics of each series are presented in Table 4.3. The means of the variables show considerable variation, ranging from a high of 0.089 for the current account deficit (D) to a low of 0.010 for the money supply (M), with the intermediate rankings being in order from highest to lowest, the interest rate (R), industrial production (IP), the stock market (Q) and inflation (P). These rankings are also mostly replicated in terms of the variances. There is evidence of non-normality as indicated by the marginal significance levels of the skewness of most variables and of the kurtosis of some variables. The two right hand columns of the Table provide the minimum and maximum values of the conditional volatilities along with their dates in brackets. As expected, the stock market crash features as being the most volatile month during the study period for the stock market variable, and the early and mid-1980s feature as being the period of most volatile interest rates.

As a precursor to the final model specification, the generated conditional volatilities were tested for their order of integration in order to avoid any possible spurious regression relationships. Inspection of Figure 4.1 suggests that the variables are all stationary, however, given the non-normality of some variables it is advisable to check the correctness of this supposition. In Table 4.4 the results of unit root tests for each variable using alternatively the Dickey-Fuller (DF) and the Phillips-Perron (PP) testing methodologies are presented. While, each test strongly indicates stationarity of every variable employed in the model, as indicated by the higher DF and PP results for each variable when compared to their critical values. The magnitude of these results are, however, typical for the conditional volatility of variables, as observed by Campbell, Lo and MacKinlay (1997). Since financial theory does not contain predictions about the form of the lag structure which may be appropriate in this analysis, the model was estimated by GLS along the lines of the general-to-specific modelling strategy (see Mizon (1995)). This involved first estimating the system described in equation (4.6) with the general specified lag structure for the conditional volatility of the stock market described in equation (4.7), and then sequentially restricting the latter equation by excluding its statistically insignificant components. The final form of the equation for the conditional volatility of the stock market is presented in equation (4.10) and the estimation results are presented in Table 4.5.

Figure 4.1: Conditional Volatilities of Financial and Business Cycle Variables

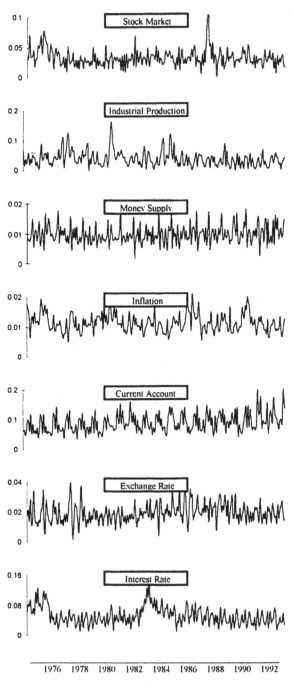

Table 4.3: Descriptive Statistics for the Conditional Volatilities of Variables Used in the Analysis

Variable	Mean	Variance	Skewness	Kurtosis	Minimum Value	Maximum Value
Q	0.033 (.00)	2.01^{e-4}	1.68 (.00)	6.78 (.00)	0.002 (88:8)	0.121 (87:12)
Y	0.039 (.00)	6.66e-4	1.48 (.00)	3.32 (.00)	0.001 (90:3)	0.164 (80:6)
M	0.010 (.00)	9.23e-6	0.50 (.00)	0.06 (.85)	0.002 (82:2)	0.018 (91:1)
P	0.011 (.00)	9.19e-6	0.62 (.00)	0.37 (.24)	0.005 (76:11)	0.023 (86:9)
D	0.089 (.00)	9.40e-4	0.79 (.00)	0.50 (.11)	0.035 (77:10)	0.201 (93:12)
E	0.019 (.00)	4.21e-5	0.52 (.00)	0.45 (.16)	0.002 (77:3)	0.040 (77:1)
R	0.053 (.00)	5.55e-4	0.84 (.00)	0.99 (.00)	0.012 (85:6)	0.148 (83:4)

Notes: The descriptive statistics are all calculated over the period 1973:8 - 1994:1. The figures in parentheses following the mean, skewness and kurtosis are the marginal significance levels for zero. The figures in parentheses following the minimum and maximum values provide the dates.

Table 4.4: Unit Root Tests of Stock Markets and Business Cycle Variables

Variable	Dickey-Fuller Test	Phillips-Perron Test
Q	-179.76	-211.69
Y	-135.43	-133.60
M	-298.61	-290.51
P	-139.18	-143.73
D	-206.29	-239.43
E	-216.13	-187.84
R	-130.03	-140.46

Notes: The tests are conducted over the period from 1974:1-1994:1 for the levels, and 1974:2-1994:1 for the conditional volatilities. The critical values are -2.57 for both tests. See Dickey and Fuller (1979), Fuller (1976), Phillips (1987) and Phillips and Perron (1988).

$$\hat{\sigma}_t^Q = \lambda_0 + \lambda_1 Crash + \lambda_2 \hat{\sigma}_{t-1}^Q + \lambda_3 \hat{\sigma}_{t-2}^Q + \lambda_4 \hat{\sigma}_{t-3}^{IP}$$
$$+ \lambda_5 \hat{\sigma}_t^M + \lambda_6 \hat{\sigma}_t^P + \lambda_7 \hat{\sigma}_{t-1}^P + \lambda_8 \hat{\sigma}_{t-1}^D + \lambda_9 \hat{\sigma}_{t-2}^D$$
$$+ \lambda_{10} \hat{\sigma}_t^E + \lambda_{11} \hat{\sigma}_{t-1}^R + \varepsilon_t$$

(4.10)

Looking firstly at the model's overall performance as presented by the equation diagnostics in the bottom part of the Table, the R^2 statistic indicates that it explains an average of 35 percent of the variation in the conditional variance of the Australian stock market, with the standard error of the estimate being equal to one third of the mean of the dependent variable. This compares well with related work of, for example, Steward (1993). The regression F-statistic is highly significant, indicating that the included variables are jointly statistically significant determinants of the conditional volatility of the Australian stock market. The Durbin-Watson (DW) and Kolmogorov-Smirnov (K-S) statistics indicate that the model is free from first and higher order autocorrelation. The $ARCH$ test for heteroscedasticity indicates that this is not a problem, which is intuitive insofar as we are working with the conditional volatilities of all variables. Finally, three versions of the Chow test for structural stability are included in the table: $CHOW^1$ splits the sample in half (from 1974:1 - 1984:12 and from 1985:1 - 1994:1), $CHOW^2$ splits it into one third and two thirds (from 1974:1 - 1981:12 and from 1982:1 1994:1), while $CHOW^3$ splits it into two thirds and one third from 1974:1-1987:12 and from 1988:1-1994:1) respectively. These test statistics confirm that the model's structure remains stable over time.

Looking next at the individual coefficient estimates of the lagged dependent variable, the λ_2 and λ_3 coefficients indicate that the model incorporates significant lagged dependent terms which implies that the volatility in the Australian stock market responds dynamically to variations in the volatility of the financial and business cycle variables. The equation also contains a positively signed and statistically significant constant term with a value of $\lambda_0 = 0.035$ and associated t-statistic of 6.07 which indicates that stock market volatility in Australia tends to proceed independently from the other influences included in the model. The dummy variable for the October 1987 stock market crash is also positively signed as expected with a coefficient of $\lambda_1 = 0.063$, and it is strongly statistically significant with a t-statistic of 5.89.

Table 4.5: GLS Estimation of the ARCH Model of Conditional Volatility of the Australian Stock Market

Explanatory Variable	Model Coefficient	Estimated Coefficient	t Statistic
Constant	λ_0	0.035	6.07
Dum87	λ_1	0.063	5.89
$\hat{\sigma}_{Q}^{-1}$	λ_2	0.123	2.24
$\hat{\sigma}_{IP}^{-2}$	λ_3	0.326	5.92
$\hat{\sigma}_{M}^{-3}$	λ_4	-0.088	3.11
$\hat{\sigma}_{P}$	λ_5	-1.093	4.41
$\hat{\sigma}_{P}$	λ_6	-0.541	2.00
$\hat{\sigma}_{D}^{-1}$	λ_7	0.853	3.09
$\hat{\sigma}_{t-1}^{D}$	λ_8	-0.064	2.53
$\hat{\sigma}_{tE2}$	λ_9	-0.088	3.46
$\hat{\sigma}_{R}$	λ_{10}	0.164	1.40
$\hat{\sigma}_{t-1}$	λ_{11}	0.078	2.42

Equation diagnostics
Estimation period 1974:1-1994:1
Observations, df 241, 229

R^2	.35
SEE	.012
SSR	.031
F(11,229)	11.80 (.00)
DW	2.21
K-S	0.12 (.10)
ARCH	0.32 (.57)
CHOW[1]	1.17 (.32)
CHOW2	1.24 (.28)
CHOW3	1.74 (.09)

Notes: SEE and SSR denote the standard error of the estimate and the sum of squared residuals. F(11,129) denotes the regression F-statistic. DW and K-S denote the Durbin-Watson statistic and the Kolmogorov-Smirnov test for higher order autocorrelation. The ARCH and CHOW tests are for heteroscedasticity and structural stability. Concerning the latter: $CHOW^1$, $CHOW^2$ and $CHOW^3$ split the sample in half, into 1/3 and 2/3, and into 2/3 and 1/3 respectively.

Turning now to examine the effects of the conditional volatility of the business cycle variables on the conditional volatility of the Australian stock market, all variables are statistically significant at the five percent level of significance except for the conditional volatility of the exchange rate. Increases in the conditional volatility of interest rates and inflation are associated with higher stock market conditional volatility, while increases in the conditional volatility of industrial production, the current account deficit and the money supply are associated with lower stock market conditional volatility. More specifically, the positive λ_{11} coefficient of 0.078 (with its t-statistic of 2.42) indicates that the conditional volatility of interest rates impacts positively upon the conditional volatility of the stock market with a one-month lag. The negative λ_6 coefficient of -0.541 (with its t-statistic of 2.00) and the positive λ_7 coefficient of 0.853 (with its t-statistic of 3.09) together imply that the conditional volatility of inflation has a net positive impact on the conditional volatility of the stock market with a one-month lag. By way of contrast, the negative λ_4 coefficient of -0.088 (with its t-statistic of 3.11) indicates that the conditional volatility of the stock market varies indirectly with the conditional volatility of industrial production with a three-month lag. As the negative λ_5 coefficient of -1.093 (with its t-statistic of 4.41) indicates, the same qualitative relationship pertains to the effect of changes in the conditional volatility of the money supply on the conditional volatility of the stock market, although in this case the strength of the relationship is greater and the impact is immediate (ie., within 1 month). Indeed, the magnitude of the λ_5 coefficient together with its associated t-statistic indicates that apart from the stock market's recent volatility history and the dummy variable for the October 1987 stock market crash, the most significant determinant of volatility in the Australian stock market is the degree of volatility which exists in the money supply.

Turning to the effects of the conditional volatility of the current account deficit on the conditional volatility of the stock market, the negative λ_8 coefficient of -0.064 (with its t-statistic of 2.53) and the greater negative λ_9 coefficient of -0.088 (with its t-statistic of 3.46) together indicate an indirect relationship with a lag of up to 2 months. Perhaps one of the most interesting findings to emerge is that there is no evidence of volatility spillover from the foreign exchange market to the stock market in this low frequency analysis of the Australian data. Although the λ_{10} coefficient is positive and equal to 0.164, its t-statistic of 1.40 indicates that the relationship is not statistically significant. This finding is consistent with the work of Ratner (1993) who employed the bivariate cointegration methodology in order to examine whether the exchange rate impacts upon monthly stock prices in the US, and concluded negatively before suggesting that any such relationship is spurious if the markets operate efficiently. Our analysis, which focuses on the conditional volatility rather than on the levels of market returns, confirms the findings of Ratner (1993) in a low frequency context. Whether this finding would be replicated in higher frequency studies remains on the research agenda.

Summary and Conclusions

The purpose of this chapter has been to contribute to the literature on the causes of stock market volatility by examining the determinants of movements in the volatility of equity returns in a small, internationally integrated stock market. The Australian stock market serves as an interesting example in this regard insofar as it is increasingly integrated with the important international stock markets throughout Asia and the rest of the world. The chapter developed and estimated a model which is capable of explaining movements in the conditional volatility of the Australian All Industrials stock market index. It employed a low frequency monthly dataset including stock market returns, interest rates, inflation, the money supply, industrial production and the current account deficit over the period from July 1972 to January 1994.

The results presented in this chapter constitute new evidence which is interpretable as an extension of the low frequency analysis of Schwert (1989) who did not include international factors such as the current account deficit and the exchange rate in his investigation of the causes of stock market volatility in the US. In addition, a novel feature of the analysis presented here is the estimation strategy employed to overcome the generated regressors problem (see *inter alia*, Pagan (1984, 1986); McAleer and McKenzie (1991); and Oxley and McAleer (1993)) which yields inefficient estimates, introduces bias into a number of diagnostic test statistics and generates potentially invalid inferences. This problem is overcome here by jointly estimating the equation for the conditional volatility of the stock market returns together with the equations determining the conditional volatilities of all variables included in the model using the Generalised Least Squares (GLS) estimation procedure and the Hendry general-to-specific estimation strategy.

Amongst the most important determinants of the conditional volatility of the Australian stock market are found to be the conditional volatilities of inflation and interest rates which are directly associated with stock market volatility, and the conditional volatilities of industrial production, the current account deficit and the money supply which are indirectly associated with stock market conditional volatility. Amongst these variables, the strongest effect is found to be from the conditional volatility of the money supply to the conditional volatility of the stock market. By contrast, no evidence is found of a statistically significant relationship between the conditional volatility of the foreign exchange market and the conditional volatility of the stock market in Australia.

65

5 Monetary Volatility and Real Output Volatility: An Empirical Model of the Transmission Mechanism, Australia, Jan 1972 - Jan 1994

Introduction

It is well known that the prices of financial assets such as stocks, bonds and foreign exchange tend to exhibit greater volatility over time than many economic components of the business cycle such as real output and inflation. The traditional explanation for the volatility of financial asset prices (see, *inter alia*, Fama (1970) and Merton (1987)), which is based on the arrival of new information to the market, is well regarded by economic and financial researchers, although it is widely recognized to constitute significantly less than the whole story. For example, LeRoy and Porter (1981) and Shiller (1981) have contributed to the debate about whether some financial asset prices exhibit *excess* volatility of a degree greater than what would be expected from the time paths of asset payoff streams and discount rates. Although some researchers (especially Merton (1987) and West (1988)) have argued that much of the so-called excess volatility can be explained by the use of inappropriate econometric testing techniques, Campbell and Shiller (1988) and LeRoy and Park (1992) amongst others have corrected their testing methodologies and still found excess volatility in financial asset prices. Other explanations for the observed excess volatility of financial asset prices have emerged in recent times, including the participation of noise traders in the market (see *inter alia* Shiller (1984) and De Long et al (1990)), the existence of asymmetric information in the market (see *inter alia* Gennotte and Leland (1990) and Allen and Gorton (1993)), and liquidity trading by market participants (see Allen and Gale (1994). Campbell and Kyle (1993) overview this work and provide empirical estimates of some of the explanations of excess financial asset price volatility.

While this literature is very important in contributing to economic and financial analysts' understanding of the causes and transmission of volatility across markets and sectors of the economy, a related literature has focused on the extent to which financial volatility is capable of impacting upon the level of real macroeconomic activity. This literature has a number of constituent strands, amongst the most important of which concerns whether monetary and/or interest rate volatility is capable of impacting significantly upon the level of real output, employment and prices. Previous research on this issue has been reported by, *inter alia*, Mascaro and Meltzer (1983), Evans (1984), Belongia (1984), Tatom (1985) and McMillin (1988). The theoretical basis for the relationship is that volatile monetary growth generates volatile interest rates which raise the riskiness of bond holdings. This in turn raises the demand for money and the level of interest rates which impedes corporate investment and lowers the level of real economic activity. Most of the above-mentioned researchers find evidence of significant linkage from either monetary or interest rate volatility to the level of real economic performance, although Evans (1984) finds evidence only from interest rate volatility rather than from monetary volatility. The most general of these studies by McMillan (1988) allows both monetary and interest rate volatility to influence a set of macroeconomic variables, and reports that monetary growth volatility has strong effects on interest rates, the level of real output and prices.

The purpose of this chapter is to contribute to the literature on the extent to which monetary growth volatility is transmitted to the real sector of the macroeconomy. Using a monthly Australian dataset including the money supply, the interest rate, the share market, the foreign exchange rate, inflation and real output over the period from January 1972 to January 1994, this chapter formulates and estimates an empirical model which examines the extent to which variations in the volatility of monetary growth are transmitted to the volatility of financial asset prices, inflation and real output growth. The analysis contains some novel features. Unlike most previous related research which focuses on the transmission mechanisms from monetary volatility to the *levels* of financial asset prices and macroeconomic variables, this chapter focuses on the transmission mechanisms from monetary growth volatility to the *volatility* of financial asset prices and the volatility of macroeconomic variables. The transmission mechanism from monetary growth volatility to output volatility which operates through the volatility of financial asset prices is modeled here using a Markowitz efficient portfolio comprising bonds, stocks and foreign exchange which eliminates the diversifiable risk associated with holding these assets. This portfolio therefore contains only the systemic financial risk which cannot be diversified away by sophisticated market participants, and it is intuitive that this should be the transmission mechanism that is examined in a modern financial system. By way of comparison, a second version of the model is presented which retains each of the financial assets with unitary weights so that a level of diversifiable financial risk remains. Finally, as in the previous chapter, the estimation strategy employed here constitutes a generalization of the ARCH-type models of Davidian and Carroll (1987) and Schwert (1989) by jointly estimating the equations which describe the monetary growth volatility transmission mechanisms together with the equations which generate the conditional volatilities of all variables included in the model using the Generalised Least

Squares (GLS) estimation procedure together with the Hendry general-to-specific estimation strategy (see Mizon (1995) for a recent overview).

The chapter is structured as follows. The next Section describes the dataset together with the methodology which is used to measure the conditional volatilities. Following this the model estimation results concerning the monetary volatility transmission mechanism are discussed. Finally the chapter presents a summary and draws together the main conclusions.

Data and Measurement of Conditional Volatility

In order to efficiently describe the measurement of volatility which will be used in the empirical tests, it is appropriate to first describe the dataset. The money supply (M) is measured by the quantity of M1, the bond rate of interest (R) is on three-month bank accepted bills, the return on equity is the percentage change in the Australian *All Industrials Sharemarket Index* (Q), the return on foreign exchange (S) is the percentage change in the spot Australian / US dollar exchange rate, the level of real output (Y) is the index of industrial production, and the price level (P) is given by the wholesale price index. All data is sampled monthly over the period January 1972 - January 1994. Table 5.1 contains a description of each variable used in the analysis together with its source.

From these variables we construct another variable, financial volatility (FIN), which comprises the degree of systemic undiversifiable volatility in a portfolio of financial assets drawn from the share market, the bond market and the foreign exchange market. The variable FIN is generated as the solution to the Markowitz-efficient minimum variance portfolio selection problem (with short sales allowed and no riskless borrowing or lending). The efficient portfolio is as follows.

$$\text{FIN}_t = 0.939 \Delta Log(Q)_t + 0.021 \Delta Log(R)_t + 0.040 \Delta Log(S)_t \quad (5.1)$$

An obviously interesting aspect of this portfolio in the current analysis is that it contains the residual undiversifiable risk within the group of financial assets that comprises it, and it is variations in this systemic financial risk that we shall in due course model as an important element of the transmission mechanism that links *monetary growth volatility* to the *volatility of real output and prices*. It is noticeable that the asset weights in the efficient portfolio in (5.1) are all positive, with the share market return dominating both the bond interest rate and the return on foreign exchange. In order to generate the conditional volatilities, we begin by obtaining monthly estimates of the standard deviations of the relevant variables.

68

Table 5.1: Variables Used and Data Sources

R: The interest rate on 3-month bank accepted bills in Australia, sampled at the end of the last trading day each month. Source is *Reserve Source Bank of Australia*.

Q: Australian sharemarket All Industrials Index, sampled on close of trading on the last trading day in the month. The index is re-based to 1973=100. Source is Australian Stock Exchange.

S: The spot exchange rate of the Australian - US dollar exchange rate, sampled at the end of the last trading day each month. Source is *OECD Economic Database*.

FIN: The Markowitz efficient minimum variance portfolio comprising 93.9 percent in the share market, 4.0 percent in the foreign exchange market and 2.1 percent in the bond market. The index is re-based to 1973=100. Source is the previous three variables.

P: The monthly index of wholesale prices in Australia, re-based to 1973=100. Source is *OECD Economic Database*.

I: The monthly percentage change in the wholesale price index (*P*) in Australia., re-based to 1973=100. Source is *OECD Economic Database*.

Y: The monthly percentage change in the index of industrial production, rebased to 1973=100. Source is *OECD Economic Database*.

D87: Dummy variable to capture the effects of the October 1987 stock market crash. It takes the value of 1 in October 1987 and 0 at all other times.

SD: Monthly seasonal dummy variables to capture the effects of monthly variations the conditional mean and conditional standard deviations of the business cycle and financial variables.

The approach adopted here is to employ the methodology of Davidian and Carroll (1987) as used in Chapter four of this book. Let X denote the vector of variables employed in the study including money, financial asset prices, the price level and real output, ie., $X = X$ *(M, R, Q, S, P, Y)*, let σ_t^x denote the unconditional standard deviation of these variables, and let

$$\hat{\sigma}_t^x = E_t(\sigma_t^x / I_{t-1})$$ denote the corresponding conditional standard deviations.

The latter are obtained as $\overset{\wedge}{\sigma}{}_t^x = \sigma_t^x - \varepsilon_{2,t}^x$ from the following regression,

$$\sigma_t^x = \beta_1(H)\sigma_t^x + \sum_{m=1}^{12}\beta_m SD_{m,t} + \varepsilon_{2,t}^x \qquad (5.2)$$

where $\beta_1(H)$ and SD_m's are as previously defined on pp.77 and $\sigma_t^x = /\varepsilon_{1,t}^x/$ where

$$\varepsilon_{1,t}^x = \Delta Log(X)_t - E_t(\Delta Log(X)_t / I_{t-1})$$

$$= \Delta Log(X)_t - \alpha_1(H)\Delta Log(X)_t - \sum_{m=1}^{12}\alpha_m SD_{m,t} \qquad (5.3)$$

and $\alpha_1(H)$ is another 12th order polynomial in the lag operator H. The measure of conditional volatility in equation (5.2) to (5.3) replicates equations (4.4) to (4.5) as employed in Chapter four.

Table 5.2 presents the summary statistics from the OLS estimates of the 12 autoregressions contained in equations (5.2) and (5.3) applied to each of the variables in the X vector which are used as inputs during the GLS estimation procedure. Looking firstly at the top part of the Table which summarizes the equations for the conditional means, the equations explain between 7 and 79 percent of the variation in the dependent variables, with, as expected, the financial variables (including the interest rate, the share market returns and the foreign exchange rate) occupying the lower end of the explanatory power rankings. The equations are all free from higher order autocorrelation as evidenced by the Ljung-Box Q-statistics. The sums of the lagged dependent coefficients (with their marginal significance levels in brackets) are presented in the fourth column of the Table under the heading of *Sum*. The columns headed by F_1 and F_2 provide the F-statistics for the joint exclusion of, respectively, all lagged dependents and all the seasonal variables in each regression. The lagged dependents in the equations for the share market and inflation are jointly significant in their respective equations, while the seasonal dummy variables are jointly significant in all equations except those for inflation and the exchange rate. With regard to the Australian share market, the latter finding is in conformity with other researchers such as Gultekin and Gultekin (1983) who found statistically significant share market seasonality in 14 out of 17 countries studied, Kramer (1994) who related stock market seasonality in the US to underlying macroeconomic seasonality, and Haugen and Jorian (1996) who have reported that the January effect has not declined in size during the past three decades in the US. Looking next at the bottom part of the Table which summarizes the equations for the conditional standard deviations, the equations explain predictably less of the variation in the dependent variables, and all are free from higher order autocorrelation as evidenced by the Ljung-Box Q-statistics. The lagged dependents in the equations for the interest rate, the stock market, inflation and industrial production are jointly significant in their respective equations, while the seasonal dummy variables are, as in the top part of the table, jointly significant in the equations for all variables except the exchange rate and inflation. Figure 5.1 presents time series plots of the conditional volatilities of all variables used in the study. Most series display considerable time variation in their volatilities. Of particular note is the high volatility of interest rates during the 1980s and the share market volatility associated with the October 1987 crash. The summary statistics of each series are presented in Table 5.3. The means of the variables show considerable variation, ranging from a high of 0.053 for the interest rate (R) to a low of 0.010 for the money supply (M), with the intermediate rankings being in order from highest to lowest, the share market (Q), the financial asset portfolio (FIN) together with real output (Y), and the price level (P). These rankings are also mostly replicated in terms of the variances. There is evidence of non-normality as indicated by the marginal significance levels of the skewness of most variables and of the kurtosis of some variables. The two right hand columns of the table provide the minimum and maximum values of the conditional volatilities along with their dates in brackets. As expected, the stock market crash features as being the most volatile month during the study period for the stock market variable, and the early and mid-1980s feature as being the period of most volatile interest rates.

In order to avoid any possible spurious regression relationships the generated conditional volatilities were tested for their order of integration. Inspection of Figure 5.1 suggests that the variables are all stationary, to check the correctness of this supposition, Table 5.4 presents the results of the unit root tests for each variable using alternatively the Dickey-Fuller (DF) and the Phillips-Perron (PP) testing methodologies. As expected, each test strongly indicates stationarity of every variable employed in the model. Although the DF and PP test results appear high compared to their critical values, the magnitude of these tests are typical of unit root tests for the conditional volatilities of variables.

71

Table 5.2: **Estimation Results of the ARCH Models of Monetary, Financial and Business Cycle Conditional Volatility, July 1970 - January 1994**

Variable	R^2	SEE	Q	Sum	F_1	F_2

$$X_t = \sum_{j=1}^{12} \delta_j^x X_{t-j} - \sum_{m=1}^{12} \eta_m SD_{m,t} + \xi_t^x$$

Variable	R^2	SEE	Q	Sum	F_1	F_2
M	.62	.014	30.44 (.73)	0.33 (1.90)	1.72 (.06)	10.39 (.00)*
R	.21	.081	22.77 (.96)	0.31 (1.69)	1.74 (.06)	2.52 (.00)*
Q	.21	.047	51.05 (.05)*	-3.81 (6.05)*	35.82 (.00)*	2.43 (.01)*
S	.07	.030	20.43 (.98)	-0.02 (0.10)	1.20 (.29)	0.47 (.93)
FIN	.20	.044	23.10 (.95)	0.28 (1.80)	4.05 (.00)*	1.72 (.06)
P	.22	.016	20.27 (.98)	0.42 (2.89)*	4.74 (.00)*	1.34 (.20)
Y	.79	.062	24.20 (.93)	-0.90 (0.01)	1.75 (.06)	2.83 (.00)*

$$\sigma_t^x = \sum_{j=1}^{12} \alpha_j^x \sigma_{t-j}^x + \sum_{m=1}^{12} \beta_m SD_{m,t} + \varepsilon_t^x$$

Variable	R^2	SEE	Q	Sum	F_1	F_2
M	.10	.009	25.85 (.89)	0.22 (1.10)	0.94 (.51)	2.54 (.00)*
R	.17	.054	19.95 (.99)	0.62 (4.83)*	2.83 (.00)*	1.97 (.03)*
Q	.20	.029	19.04 (.99)	0.49 (3.70)*	4.00 (.00)*	1.91 (.03)*
S	.08	.023	26.81 (.87)	0.33 (1.87)	1.12 (.34)	1.68 (.07)
FIN	.21	.027	19.57 (.99)	0.48 (3.61)*	4.09 (.00)*	2.02 (.02)*
P	.07	.011	29.92 (.75)	0.34 (2.15)*	1.02(.43)	1.74 (.06)
Y	.32	.039	21.37 (.97)	0.55 (4.82)*	6.20 (.00)*	3.35 (.00)*

Note: The Table presents the regression summary results for equations (5.2) and (5.3) in the text, regressed on each variable in the Table. *SEE* denotes the standard error of the regression and *Q* denotes the Ljung-Box test for higher order autocorrelation. *Sum* denotes the sums of coefficients of the lagged dependent variables in each regression equation. F_1 denotes the F-statistics for the joint exclusion of all lagged dependents in each regression. F_2 denotes the F-statistics for the joint exclusion of all the seasonal coefficients in each regression. Marginal significance levels for these test statistics are presented in the brackets.

Model Estimates and Results

In order to appropriately account for the non-zero cross equation covariances which arise from the generated regressors problem (see, *inter alia*, Pagan (1984, 1986); McAleer and McKenzie (1991); and Oxley and McAleer (1993)), the equations explaining the transmission of monetary growth volatility to the volatility of financial asset prices, inflation and real output are estimated jointly with the equations determining the conditional volatilities of all variables included in the model using the Generalised Least Squares (GLS) estimation procedure together with the Hendry general-to-specific estimation strategy (see Mizon (1995) for an overview). This procedure is fully described in chapter four, section 3. In summary, we first stack the system to be estimated in the following form with N equations and T observations:

$$\begin{bmatrix} y_1 \\ y_n \end{bmatrix} = \begin{bmatrix} X_1 & \cdots & 0 \\ 0 & \cdots & X_n \end{bmatrix} \begin{bmatrix} \beta_1 \\ \beta_n \end{bmatrix} + \begin{bmatrix} \varepsilon_1 \\ \varepsilon_n \end{bmatrix} \tag{5.4}$$

where y is an $NT \times 1$ vector of dependent variables, X is an $NT \times (\sum_{i=1}^{M} K_i)$ matrix of explanatory variables as in equation (5.2), β is an $NT \times (\sum_{i=1}^{M} K_i)$ matrix of coefficients and ε is an $NT \times 1$ vector of errors. Writing the system in matrix form as in equation (5.5), we can describe the GLS estimator as given by equation (5.6):

$$y = X\beta + \varepsilon \tag{5.5}$$

$$\hat{\beta} = (X'\Omega^{-1}X)^{-1}X'\Omega^{-1}y. \tag{5.6}$$

Version 1: Modeling the Transmission of Monetary Volatility Through the Markowitz Efficient Portfolio of Financial Assets

In this version of the model which aggregates the share market, the bond market and the foreign exchange market into the Markowitz efficient portfolio of financial assets, *FIN*, the X vector takes the form of $X^l = X^l$ *(M, FIN, P, Y)* in

73

equation (5.4) which now contains 11 equations (i.e., $N = 11$) with 259 observations (i.e., $T = 259$) on each variable. The first four of these equations are given by (5.2) for each variable in the X^l vector, the second four equations are given by (5.3) for each variable in the X^l vector, and the final three equations take the following form for the last three variables (ie., FIN, P and Y) in the X^l vector.

$$\hat{\sigma}_t^{X^l} = \lambda_0 + \lambda_1(K_1)\hat{\sigma}_t^{X^l} + \lambda_2(K_2)\hat{\sigma}_t^{M}$$
$$+ \lambda_3 D87 + \varepsilon_t^{X^l} \tag{5.7}$$

where the $\lambda_1(K_1)$ and $\lambda_2(K_2)$ are polynomials of the 4th degree in the lag operators, K_1 and K_2 respectively. Equation (5.7) relates the conditional volatilities of the return on the Markowitz efficient portfolio of financial assets, inflation and real output to these variables, the conditional volatility of monetary growth and the dummy variable to capture any effects associated with the October 1987 stock market crash which is clearly visible in Figure 5.1.

The final form of the equations for the conditional volatilities of the financial asset prices, inflation and real output is given in equations (5.8) to (5.10) below.

$$\hat{\sigma}_t^{FIN} = \lambda_0 + \lambda_1 D87 + \lambda_2 \hat{\sigma}_{t-1}^{FIN} + \lambda_3 \hat{\sigma}_{t-2}^{FIN}$$
$$+ \lambda_4 \hat{\sigma}_t^{P} + \lambda_5 \hat{\sigma}_{t-3}^{P} + \lambda_6 \hat{\sigma}_t^{M} + \lambda_7 \hat{\sigma}_{t-4}^{M} + \varepsilon_t^{FIN} \tag{5.8}$$

$$\hat{\sigma}_t^{P} = \lambda_0 + \lambda_1 \hat{\sigma}_{t-1}^{P} + \lambda_2 \hat{\sigma}_{t-4}^{P} + \lambda_3 (\hat{\sigma}_{t-2}^{Y} - \hat{\sigma}_{t-3}^{Y})$$
$$+ \lambda_4 \hat{\sigma}_t^{FIN} + \lambda_5 \hat{\sigma}_{t-1}^{FIN} + \lambda_6 \hat{\sigma}_{t-2}^{FIN} + \lambda_{71} \hat{\sigma}_t^{M} \tag{5.9}$$
$$+ \lambda_8 \hat{\sigma}_{t-2}^{M} + \varepsilon_t^{P}$$

74

$$\hat{\sigma}_t^Y = \lambda_0 + \lambda_1 \hat{\sigma}_{t-1}^Y + \lambda_2 \hat{\sigma}_{t-3}^P + \lambda_3 \hat{\sigma}_t^{FIN}$$
$$+ \lambda_4 \hat{\sigma}_t^M + \varepsilon_t^Y \qquad (5.10)$$

The estimation results for these equations are presented in Table 5.5. Looking firstly at the model's overall performance as presented by the equation diagnostics in the bottom part of the Table, the R^2 statistics indicate that the constituent equations explain between 38 percent (for the conditional volatility of inflation) and 27 percent (for the conditional volatility of the financial asset returns) of the variation in the dependent variables, with the standard errors of the estimates (*SEE*) and the sums of squared residuals (*SSR*) being respectable given the means of the dependent variables (*MDV*). The regression F-statistics are all highly significant, indicating that the included variables are all jointly statistically significant determinants of the dependent variables in each equation. Two tests for autocorrelation are reported at the bottom of the Table, namely, the Durbin-Watson (*DW*) statistic which tests for first order autocorrelation and the Kolmogorov-Smirnov (*K-S*) statistic which tests for higher order autocorrelation, with both tests indicating that autocorrelation does not seem to be a problem in the model. The *ARCH* test for heteroscedasticity indicates that this is not a problem in any of the equations except for the equation for the conditional volatility of real output. Finally, three versions of the Chow test for structural stability are included in the Table; $CHOW_1$ splits the sample in half (from 1974:1 - 1984:12 and from 1985:1 - 1994:1), $CHOW_2$ splits it into one third and two thirds (from 1974:1 - 1981:12 and from 1982:1 1994:1), while $CHOW_3$ splits it into two thirds and one third (from 1974:1 - 1987:12 and from 1988:1 - 1994:1) respectively. These test statistics confirm that the model's structure remains stable over time.

Looking next at the individual coefficient estimates, it is noticeable from inspection of the λ_0 terms that all three equations have statistically significant constant terms, while only equation (8) for the conditional volatility of the financial asset returns has a statistically significant dummy variable to capture the effects of the October 1987 stock market crash. This is an interesting finding insofar as it demonstrates that the extraordinary stock market volatility associated with the crash did not significantly spill over into any other non-financial domestic markets. Also, the statistically significant lagged dependent variables in each equation indicate that the responses of the dependent variables to variations in the conditional volatilities of the explanatory variables occur dynamically over time, ranging from a one-month lag in equation (5.10) to a four-month lag in equation (5.9).

Figure 5.1: Conditional Volatilities of Financial and Economic Variables

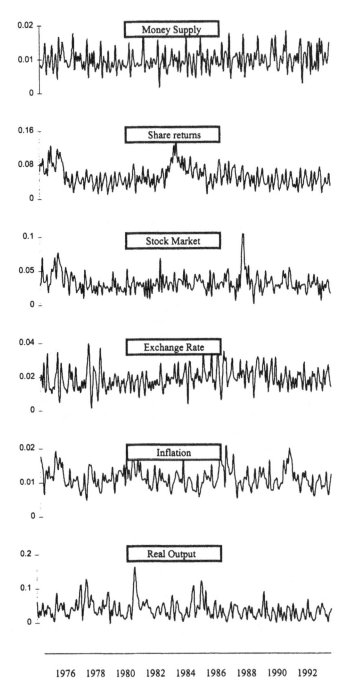

Table 5.3: Descriptive Statistics for the Conditional Volatilities of Variables Used in the Analysis

Variable	Mean	Variance	Skewness	Kurtosis	Minimum Value	Maximum Value
M	0.010 (.00)	9.23^{e-6}	0.50 (.00)	0.06 (.85)	0.002 (82:2)	0.018 (91:1)
R	0.053 (.00)	5.55e-4	0.84 (.00)	0.99 (.00)	0.012 (85:6)	0.148 (83:4)
Q	0.033 (.00)	2.01e-4	1.68 (.00)	6.78 (.00)	0.002 (88:8)	0.121 87:12)
S	0.019 (.00)	4.21e-5	0.52 (.00)	0.45 (.16)	0.002 (77:3)	0.040 (77:1)
FIN	0.031 (.00)	1.81e-4	1.81 (.00)	7.75 (.00)	0.001 (88:8)	0.117 (87:12)
P	0.011 (.00)	9.19e-6	0.62 (.00)	0.37 (.24)	0.005 (76:11)	0.023 (86:9)
Y	0.039 (.00)	6.66e-4	1.48 (.00)	3.32 (.00)	0.001 (90:3)	0.164 (80:6)

Notes: The descriptive statistics are all calculated over the period 1973:8 - 1994:1. The figures in parentheses following the mean, skewness and kurtosis are the marginal significance levels for zero. The figures in parentheses following the minimum and maximum values provide the dates.

Table 5.4: Unit Root Tests of Stock Markets and Business Cycle Variables

Variable	Dickey-Fuller Test	Phillips-Perron Test
Q	-179.76	-211.69
Y	-135.43	-133.60
M	-298.61	-290.51
P	-139.18	-143.73
D	-206.29	-239.43
E	-216.13	-187.84
R	-130.03	-140.46
ECO	-227.97	-201.76
FIN	-180.30	-208.88
SYS	-175.91	-202.28

Notes: The tests are conducted over the period from 1974:1-1994:1 for the levels, and 1974:2-1994:1 for the conditional volatilities. The critical values are -2.57 for both tests. See Dickey and Fuller (1979), Fuller (1976), Phillips (1987) and Phillips and Perron (1988).

Turning now to examine the individual equations in somewhat greater detail, we begin by focusing on equation (5.8) which provides the results for the conditional volatility of the financial asset returns. In addition to the constant term, the dummy variable for the October 1987 sharemarket crash and the lagged dependent variables, this equation contains terms including the conditional volatility of inflation and the money supply, but does not include the conditional volatility of real output. More specifically, the statistically significant and negative λ_4 coefficient together with the significantly positive λ_5 coefficient provides unclear evidence of the direction of the association between the conditional volatility of inflation and the conditional volatility of the return on financial assets. By contrast, however, the statistically significant and negatively signed λ_6 and λ_7 coefficients imply that the conditional volatility of financial asset returns is negatively related to the conditional volatility of monetary growth.

Looking now at the conditional volatility of inflation equation (5.9), the statistically significant and positively signed λ_3 coefficient shows that it varies directly with the conditional volatility of real output, while the mixed signs and magnitudes of the λ_4, λ_5 and λ_6 coefficients reveal the intuitive result that the conditional volatility of financial asset returns does not impact greatly on the conditional volatility of inflation. The statistically significant and negative λ_7 coefficient together with the greater in magnitude and positively signed λ_8 coefficient imply, however, that the conditional volatility of inflation responds positively to the conditional volatility of monetary growth.

Finally, equation (5.10) shows that the conditional volatility of real output varies directly with the conditional volatility of inflation and monetary growth, and inversely with the conditional volatility of financial asset returns. The finding of a positive relationship between the conditional volatility of real output and the conditional volatility of prices in equations (5.9) and (5.10) is interesting in the light of the recent literature on the relationship between these variables in the US economy. The stylized facts are mostly agreed upon (see *inter alia*, De Long and Summers (1986); Romer (1986,1989); Taylor (1986); Balke and Gordon (1989); and Gray and Kandil (1991)) that prices have become less flexible while the level of real output has also become less volatile. The attention devoted to this issue is not surprising, given that the standard Keynesian model predicts that lower price flexibility should raise the volatility of real output. A number of authors (including Driskill and Shefrin (1986); DeLong and Summers (1986); King (1988); Chadha (1989); and Gray and Kandil (1991)) have sought to explain this stylized fact. For example, DeLong and Summers (1986) demonstrate that using an amended Taylor (1979) model, reduced wage flexibility can lead to lower real output volatility in the presence of aggregate demand shocks. The more recent work of Gray and Kandil (1991), however,

Table 5.5: **GLS Estimates of the Effects of Monetary Conditional Volatility on Financial Asset Price, Inflation and Real Output Conditional Volatility**

Coeficient	Financial Assets (8)	Inflation (9)	Real Output (10)
λ_0	0.034 (6.93)	0.003 (2.39)	0.001 (9.35)
$\lambda 1$	0.054 (4.93)	0.486 (9.31)	0.481 (8.60)
$\lambda 2$	0.271 (4.70)	0.147 (2.82)	0.869 (1.82)
$\lambda 3$	0.266 (4.65)	0.023 (3.99)	-0.208 (1.91)
$\lambda 4$	-1.397 (5.12)	-0.065 (5.20)	1.588 (3.30)
$\lambda 5$	-1.220 (4.43)	0.051 (4.19)	
$\lambda 6$	-1.136 (4.75)	0.031 (2.49)	
$\lambda 7$	-0.426 (1.83)	-0.132 (2.45)	
$\lambda 8$		0.227 (4.35)	
		Equation Diagnostics	
R^2	0.30	0.38	0.27
MDV	0.31	0.11	0.039
SEE	0.011	0.002	0.022
SSR	0.030	0.001	0.118
F(11,229)	13.25 (.00)	18.55 (.00)	21.64 (.00)
DW	2.26	2.00	2.00
LM	21.92 (.00)	20.08 (.00)	7.70 (.26)
K-S	0.10 (.10)	0.07 (.10)	0.06 (.10)
ARCH	0.15 (.70)	0.01 (.93)	26.43 (.00)
CHOW1	0.74 (.60)	0.57 (.73)	1.55 (.18)
CHOW2	1.04 (.40)	0.34 (.89)	1.26 (.28)
CHOW3	1.73 (.13)	1.50 (.19)	2.15 (.06)

Notes: *SEE* and *SSR* denote the standard error of the estimate and the sum of squared residuals. *F(11,129)* denotes the regression F-statistic. *DW* and *K-S* denote the Durbin-Watson statistic and the Kolmogorov-Smirnov test for higher order autocorrelation. The *ARCH* and *CHOW* tests are for heteroscedasticity and structural stability. *CHOW₁* splits the sample in half (from 1974:1-1984:12 and from 1985:1-1994:1), *CHOW₂* splits it into 1/3 and 2/3 (from 1974:1- 1981:12 and from 1982:1-1994:1), while *CHOW₃* splits it into 2/3 and 1/3 (from 1974:1-1987:12 and from 1988:1-1994:1) respectively.

79

endogenizes the degree of price flexibility and shows that the relationship can go either way, depending upon the nature of the exogenous shocks which impact upon them. The findings in this chapter support the existence of a positive relationship between these variables, and also supports the view of DeLong and Summers (1986) as to the reason for this, given that Smith and Murphy (1994) have employed an error correction model together with a macroeconometric model to examine the important causes of fluctuations in the Australian macroeconomy and reported that world variables accounted for little of the fluctuations in the domestic economy, the effects being dominated by variations in the level of domestic demand and real wages.

Overall, therefore, Table 5.5 provides interesting evidence of how monetary volatility gets transmitted across the various sectors of the economy. Specifically, an increase (decrease) in conditional monetary volatility brings about a decrease (increase) in financial asset price volatility through equation (5.8) and an increase (decrease) in the conditional volatility of inflation through equation (5.9). The combined effects of these changes impact upon the conditional volatility of real output through equation (5.10); the higher conditional monetary volatility directly raises real output conditional volatility, and this effect is backed up by lower financial asset price conditional volatility together with higher inflation volatility.

Version 2: The Transmission Mechanism Through Individual Financial Assets

In this version of the model which disaggregates the Markowitz efficient portfolio of financial assets into its constituent parts, namely, the share market, the bond market and the foreign exchange market, the X vector takes the form of $X^2 = X^2$ (M, R, Q, S, P, Y) in equation (5.4) which now contains 17 equations (ie., $N = 17$) with 259 observations (ie., $T = 259$) on each variable. The first six of these equations are now given by (5.2) for each variable in the X^2 vector, the second six equations are given by (5.3) for each variable in the X^2 vector, and the final five equations take the following form after estimating the system as before by GLS together with the general-to-specific estimation strategy.

$$
\begin{aligned}
\hat{\sigma}_t^R = {} & \lambda_0 + \lambda_1 \hat{\sigma}_{-1}^R + \lambda_2 \hat{\sigma}_{t-2}^R + \lambda_3 \hat{\sigma}_{t-3}^R + \lambda_4 \hat{\sigma}_{t-4}^R \\
& + \lambda_5 \hat{\sigma}_t^P + \lambda_6 (\hat{\sigma}_{t-1}^P - \hat{\sigma}_{t-3}^P) + \lambda_7 \hat{\sigma}_{t-4}^P + \lambda_8 (\hat{\sigma}_t^Y - \hat{\sigma}_{t-1}^Y) \\
& + \lambda_9 (\hat{\sigma}_{t-3}^Y - \hat{\sigma}_{t-4}^Y) + \lambda_{10} \hat{\sigma}_t^S + \lambda_{11} \hat{\sigma}_{t-2}^S + \lambda_{12} \hat{\sigma}_{t-2}^M \\
& + \lambda_{13} \hat{\sigma}_{t-4}^M + \varepsilon_t^R
\end{aligned}
\tag{5.11}
$$

$$\hat{\sigma}_t^Q = \lambda_0 + \lambda_1 D87 + \lambda_2 \hat{\sigma}_{t-1}^Q + \lambda_3 \hat{\sigma}_{t-2}^Q + \lambda_4(\hat{\sigma}_t^P - \hat{\sigma}_{t-1}^P)$$
$$+ \lambda_5 \hat{\sigma}_t^Y + \lambda_6 \hat{\sigma}_{t-3}^Y + \lambda_7 \hat{\sigma}_t^R + \lambda_8 \hat{\sigma}_t^M + \lambda_9 \hat{\sigma}_{t-4}^M + \varepsilon_t^Q \qquad (5.12)$$

$$\hat{\sigma}_t^S = \lambda_0 + \lambda_1 \hat{\sigma}_{t-1}^S + \lambda_2 \hat{\sigma}_{t-2}^S + \lambda_3 \hat{\sigma}_{t-1}^P + \lambda_4 \hat{\sigma}_{t-3}^P$$
$$+ \lambda_5(\hat{\sigma}_{t-3}^Y - \hat{\sigma}_{t-4}^Y) + \lambda_6(\hat{\sigma}_t^R - \hat{\sigma}_{t-1}^R) + \lambda_7 \hat{\sigma}_{t-3}^Q \qquad (5.13)$$
$$+ \lambda_8(\hat{\sigma}_{t-1}^M - \hat{\sigma}_{t-3}^M) + \varepsilon_t^S$$

$$\hat{\sigma}_t^P = \lambda_0 + \lambda_1 \hat{\sigma}_{-1}^P + \lambda_2 \hat{\sigma}_{t-3}^P + \lambda_3 \hat{\sigma}_{t-4}^P + \lambda_4(\hat{\sigma}_{t-2}^Y - \hat{\sigma}_{t-3}^Y)$$
$$+ \lambda_5 \hat{\sigma}_{t-4}^Y + \lambda_6 \hat{\sigma}_t^R + \lambda_7 \hat{\sigma}_{t-2}^R + \lambda_{81} \hat{\sigma}_{t-3}^R + \lambda_9(\hat{\sigma}_t^Q - \hat{\sigma}_{t-1}^Q) \qquad (5.14)$$
$$+ \lambda_{10} \hat{\sigma}_t^M + \lambda_{11} \hat{\sigma}_{t-2}^M + \lambda_{12} \hat{\sigma}_{t-4}^M + \varepsilon_t^P$$

$$\hat{\sigma}_t^Y = \lambda_0 + \lambda_1 \hat{\sigma}_{-1}^Y + \lambda_2 \hat{\sigma}_{t-1}^P + \lambda_3 \hat{\sigma}_{t-4}^P + \lambda_4 \hat{\sigma}_t^R \qquad (5.15)$$
$$+ \lambda_5 \hat{\sigma}_{t-4}^R + \lambda_6 \hat{\sigma}_t^Q + \lambda_7 \hat{\sigma}_T^m + \varepsilon_T^y$$

Table 5.6 contains the estimation results for equations (5.11) to (5.15). Looking firstly at the model's overall performance as presented by the equation diagnostics in the bottom part of the Table, the R^2 statistic indicates that the constituent equations explain between 50 percent (for the conditional volatility of the interest rate and the exchange rate) and 29 percent (for the conditional volatility of real output) of the variation in the dependent variables, with the standard errors of the estimates (*SEE*) and the sums of squared residuals (*SSR*) being respectable given the means of the dependent variables (*MDV*). The regression *F*-statistics are all highly significant, indicating that the included variables are all jointly statistically significant determinants of the dependent variables in each equation. Three tests for autocorrelation are reported at the bottom of the Table, namely, the Durbin-Watson (*DW*) statistic which tests for first order autocorrelation and the Lagrange multiplier (*LM*) test together with the Kolmogorov-Smirnov (*K-S*) statistic which both test for higher order autocorrelation. Overall, the model performs tolerably well in terms of its autocorrelation properties, with the exception of the *LM* statistics in the equations for the conditional volatility of the interest rate and the stock market which indicate the presence of some higher order autocorrelation in these equations.

Table 5.6: GLS Estimates of the Effects of Monetary Conditional Volatility on the Conditional Volatility of Interest Rates, the Share Market, the Exchange Rate, Inflation and Real Output

Co-efficient	Interest Rate (11)	Stock Market (12)	Exchange Rate (13)	Inflation (14)	Real Output (15)
λ_0	-0.019 (2.28)	0.035 (8.28)	0.021 (9.35)	0.003 (2.34)	-0.002 (0.20)
$\lambda 1$	0.243 (4.75)	0.057 (5.11)	0.223 (4.10)	0.488 (10.15)	0.484 (8.88)
$\lambda 2$	0.139 (2.64)	0.208 (3.67)	-0.274 (5.05)	-0.109 (2.06)	-0.953 (2.00)
$\lambda 3$	0.246 (4.33)	0.261 (4.77)	0.322 (2.50)	0.311 (5.75)	1.782 (3.50)
$\lambda 4$	0.154 (3.09)	-1.266 (5.24)	-0.560 (4.59)	0.025 (4.79)	0.360 (5.24)
$\lambda 5$	3.776 (10.28)	-0.055 (1.94)	-0.054 (3.95)	0.012 (2.20)	-0.179 (2.58)
$\lambda 6$	-1.732 (5.24)	-0.077 (2.67)	0.099 (6.76)	0.072 (10.67)	-0.291 (2.88)
$\lambda 7$	-2.810 (7.64)	0.086 (2.60)	0.061 (2.47)	-0.024 (3.36)	1.273 (2.64)
$\lambda 8$	0.176 (4.87)	-1.051 (4.24)	0.304 (3.60)	-0.033 (4.63)	
$\lambda 9$	0.116 (2.92)	-0.695 (2.85)	-0.039 (4.84)		
$\lambda 10$	0.678 (4.31)			-0.142 (3.01)	
$\lambda 11$	0.529 (3.37)			0.296 (6.00)	
$\lambda 12$	-1.514 (4.04)			-0.198 (4.17)	
$\lambda 13$	1.121 (3.35)				

Equation Diagnostics

R^2	.50	.33	.50	.46	.29
MDV	.053	.033	.053	.011	.039
SEE	.002	.012	.017	.002	.022
SSR	.017	.032	.067	.001	.114
F(11,229)	20.28 (.00)	13.50 (.00)	11.39 (.00)	17.52(.00)	14.79 (.00)
DW	2.03	2.23	2.03	2.01	1.98
LM	12.89 (.01)	16.30 (.00)	2.93 (.57)	7.60 (.11)	5.81 (.44)
K-S	.11(.10)	.10 (.10)	.09 (.10)	.09 (.10)	.04 (.10)
ARCH	.01 (.93)	.05 (.83)	.45 (.50)	.20 (.66)	22.17 (.00)
CHOW	1.64 (.11)	1.19 (.32)	3.85 (.00)	1.89 (.05)	1.45 (.19)

Notes: *SEE* and *SSR* denote the standard error of the estimate and the sum of squared residuals. *F(11,129)* denotes the regression F-statistic. *DW* and *K-S* denote the Durbin-Watson statistic and the Kolmogorov-Smirnov test for higher order autocorrelation. The *ARCH* and *CHOW* tests are for heteroscedasticity and structural stability.

With regard to the effects of monetary volatility, however, the statistically significant λ_{12} and λ_{13} coefficients, which have opposite signs, indicate that the net effect on the conditional volatility of the interest rate is negative. It is noticeable that the conditional volatility of the share market does not feature in this equation, a result which indicates that share market volatility does not seem to cause interest rate volatility. This is consistent with the finding that the dummy variable for the October 1987 stock market crash features only in equation (5.12).

Turning the focus of attention to equation (5.12) for the conditional volatility of the share market, previous Australian research by Brailsford and Faff (1993) and Kearns and Pagan (1993) has examined the relative explanatory power of alternative models of conditional volatility, but neither has related share market volatility to the volatility of financial and/or business cycle variables or *vice versa*. In Table 5.6, however, the statistically significant and negatively signed λ_4 coefficient in equation (5.12) indicates that changes in the conditional volatility of inflation impact directly on the conditional volatility of the share market. The negatively signed and statistically significant λ_5 and λ_6 coefficients indicate that a similar relationship holds for the conditional volatility of real output, and the larger and more statistically significant negative λ_8 and λ_9 coefficients indicate that the same qualitative relationship holds between monetary volatility and share market volatility. By contrast, the positively signed and statistically significant λ_7 coefficient indicates that higher interest rate volatility tends to raise the conditional volatility of share market returns. A noticeable absence in this equation is the conditional volatility of the exchange rate which seems not to spill over to the share market. Interestingly, however, the significantly positive λ_7 coefficient in equation (5.13) for the conditional volatility of the exchange rate shows a degree of positive spillover of conditional volatility from the share market to the foreign exchange market. The greater and more significant λ_6 coefficient in equation (5.13) indicates a greater degree of conditional volatility spillover from the interest rate to the exchange rate, while the significant and positive λ_8 coefficient also indicates that monetary volatility is directly associated with foreign exchange market volatility.

Looking now at equation (5.14) for the conditional volatility of inflation, the positive λ_4 and λ_5 coefficients imply that increases in the conditional volatility of real output tend to cause higher inflation volatility, while the significantly negative λ_9 coefficient shows that share market volatility tends to be indirectly associated with the conditional volatility of inflation. The mixed λ_6, λ_7 and λ_8 coefficients and the mixed λ_{10}, λ_{11} and λ_{12} coefficients indicate that interest rate and monetary volatility have ambiguously signed effects on the conditional volatility of inflation.

Finally, equation (5.14) which describes the conditional volatility of real output shows it responding positively to variations in the conditional volatility of the interest rate (as given by the net effects of the positive λ_4 and negative λ_5

coefficients), positively to variations in monetary volatility (as given by the positive λ_7 coefficient), positively to variations in the conditional volatility of inflation (as given by the negative λ_2 and greater positive λ_3 coefficients), and negatively to variations in share market conditional volatility (as given by the negatively significant λ_9 coefficient). As with equation (5.12) for the conditional volatility of the share market, the conditional volatility of the exchange rate does not feature in this equation.

Overall, therefore, Table 5.6 provides considerable statistical evidence of volatility spillover across financial and real markets in Australia. More specifically, an increase in the conditional volatility of the money supply causes a reduction in the conditional volatility of interest rates and the share market and a rise in the conditional volatility of the exchange rate. It also causes a direct increase in the conditional volatility of real output as given by the positively signed λ_7 coefficient of 1.273 (with its associated t-statistic of 2.64) in equation (5.15) which is reported in the right hand column of the Table. Interestingly, this direct effect of variations in the conditional volatility of money on the conditional volatility of real output is very close to the same effect which was obtained in version one of the model as given by the positively signed λ_4 coefficient of 1.588 (with its associated t-statistic of 3.30) in equation (5.10) which is reported in the right hand column of Table 5.5. Concerning the indirect mechanisms through which increases in monetary volatility impulses are transmitted to real output in version two of the model, the mechanism which operates through the interest rate tends to reduce the conditional volatility of real output, that which operates through the share market tends to raise it, and that which operates through the exchange rate is statistically insignificant and consequently does not feature in the model.

Comparison of the two versions of the model reveal that the transmission mechanism of monetary volatility which operates through the share market tends to dominate that which operates through the interest rate. This can be seen by the higher weighting of the share market in the Markowitz portfolio, and it is consistent with the fact that the λ_4 coefficient in equation (5.10) is greater than its counterpart λ_7 coefficient in equation (5.15).

Summary and Conclusion

This chapter has examined the transmission mechanisms through which variations in monetary volatility are transmitted to the real sector of the macroeconomy. Using a monthly Australian dataset including the money supply, the interest rate, the share market, the foreign exchange rate, inflation and real output over the period from January 1972 to January 1994, the research presented an empirical model which detailed how monetary volatility impulses are transmitted to the volatility of financial asset prices, inflation and real output. The transmission mechanism from monetary volatility to real output volatility which operates through the volatility of financial asset prices was modeled using two versions of the model, version one employed a Markowitz efficient portfolio of bonds, stocks and foreign exchange to eliminate the diversifiable risk associated with holding these assets, while version two retained each of the financial assets with unitary weights along with their diversifiable risk. The models were estimated by GLS together with the general-to-specific estimation strategy in order to overcome the generated regressors problem which impinges upon related work which uses ARCH-type models of the Davidian and Carroll (1987) and Schwert (1989) vintage.

The main findings of the research are the following. *First*, both versions of the model yield comparable results about the monetary volatility transmission mechanism, including strong evidence of a statistically significant direct transmission mechanism from higher (lower) monetary volatility to higher (lower) real output volatility. *Second*, higher (lower) monetary volatility is associated with lower (higher) volatility of a Markowitz efficient portfolio of financial assets. *Third*, when the financial assets are included separately in the model rather than in the efficient portfolio, higher (lower) monetary volatility is associated with lower (higher) share market and interest rate volatility and with higher (lower) foreign exchange market volatility. *Fourth*, the indirect transmission mechanisms which operate through financial asset prices tend to strengthen the direct transmission mechanism which links monetary volatility to real output volatility. *Finally*, both versions of the model indicate that the transmission of monetary volatility impulses to real output occurs predominantly through the share market rather than through interest rates, with no significant effect operating through the foreign exchange market. The latter finding is of considerable interest insofar as it tends to vindicate the view that the volatility associated with floating exchange rates does not seem to spill over to real output.

6 Fiscal Financing Decisions and Exchange Rate Variability: A Multi-country Empirical Analysis

Introduction

The evidence from Chapter four suggests that no significant empirical relationship exist between foreign exchange market volatility and stock market volatility. Evidence from Chapter five gave support to the view that volatility associated with floating exchange rates does not appear to affect real output. The evidence from both chapters provided the motivation for investigating whether fiscal policy contributes to financial asset volatility, specifically exchange rate volatility. Further motivation is provided by the fact that there is little by way of recent empirical work to guide us when investigating the links between fiscal financing and exchange rate movements. This lack of empirical work contributes to the uncertainty faced by authorities when engaged fiscal financing operations, this is especially the case under a flexible exchange rate system, where a vast range of variation can exist depending on the precise specification of the underlying model.

Despite a voluminous literature on the appropriate design and implementation of fiscal policy in economies which are open to international trade in commodities, services and financial assets, the issue remains controversial. A central concern of this controversy has focused upon whether and how innovations in the stance of fiscal policy impinge upon the foreign exchange value of a country's currency. Two types of model have been employed in the relevant theoretical literature. The traditional approach (see *inter alia*, Mundell (1963), Dornbusch (1976), Branson and Buiter (1983), Kawai (1985) and Marston (1985) employs macroeconomic models which are constructed from 'postulated' behavioural relationships which purport to describe how the economy works in aggregate without explaining the behaviour of the agents who 'make up' the economy. The second type of model which has become more popular in recent years derives its important macroeconomic relationships from the microeconomic foundations of individual optimising behaviour, (see *inter alia*, Obstfeld (1981); Persson (1984); Cuddington and Vinals (1986a, 1986b);

and Frenkel and Razin (1986). Divergent results have emerged from within and between these alternative approaches, and the growth in empirical evidence has not kept pace with theoretical advancements. The purpose of this chapter is to contribute towards redressing this imbalance.

Allowing for the considerable uncertainty which pervades appropriate specification of theoretical models of how fiscal policy operates in open economies, the appropriate modelling strategy which is adopted in this chapter utilises the vector autoregressive (VAR) technique. The suitability of this approach in the current context stems from the fact that a VAR model constitutes an unrestricted reduced form of some unknown structural system of equations so, as Zellner and Palm (1974) and Zellner (1979) have demonstrated, any structural econometric model amounts to a restricted VAR model. In the present context, this procedure facilitates investigation of how fiscal financing decisions impinge upon the exchange rate in a manner which is consistent with both the 'postulated' and optimising theoretical models.

The chapter is structured as follows. Firstly, we summarise the current state of theoretical knowledge about how innovations in the stance of fiscal policy impinge upon the exchange rate. It concludes that the relationship in question is complex insofar as it is influenced by a number of factors which operate in diverse directions. Next we present econometric analysis of quarterly data from seven countries (Australia, Britain, Canada, France, Germany, Italy and the US) over the recent period of floating exchange rates from 1975(2) to 1995(2). Finally, we calculate the impulse response functions from the VAR models in order to examine the adjustment dynamics of the exchange rate to innovations in government expenditure which are financed alternatively by higher taxes, by debt creation and by monetary expansion.

The Theory

In the literature on exchange rate determination, four broad approaches to modeling have been adopted; namely, the monetary, new classical, equilibrium and macroeconomic approaches. Each of these approaches has been found wanting when put to the test of explaining real exchange rate behaviour in the 1980s and 1990s. Dornbusch (1988) provides a summary account of the experiences of each of these models in explaining exchange rate movements, and he suggests that events were too large with sharp reversals for these models to explain exchange rate movements over the period. Meese and Rogoff (1983) have also made this point, while Frankel and Meese (1987), after an extensive review of every testable implication, have reported that in virtually every respect, exchange rate behaviour largely remains unexplained. Pentecost (1993) concludes from his extensive study of the recent empirical literature which purports to test structural macroeconomic models of the exchange rate, that none of the models adequately explains either the long-run equilibrium exchange rate or its short-run dynamics for all time periods and exchange rates. A focus on two dimensions of the above models, namely 'postulated' behavioural relationships and those based on optimising behavioural relationships, provides us with an insight into the behaviour of exchange rate responses to fiscal financing decisions.

Models Based upon 'Postulated' Behavioural Relationships

The classic analyses of Mundell (1963) and Dornbusch (1976) describe a world of perfect capital mobility in which flows of international capital are unrestricted and where assets which are denominated in domestic and foreign currencies are perfectly substitutable. If a small open economy's exchange rate is market-determined in this world, a policy of fiscal expansion will create an excess demand for money which exerts upwards pressure on the domestic rate of interest and causes the exchange rate to appreciate until the trade balance deteriorates by an amount which exactly offsets the fiscal stimulus.

More recent work, however, has demonstrated the extent to which these earlier results are dependent upon the assumptions made for the specification of the models utilised.. In this vein, Dornbusch and Fischer (1980) and Boyer and Hodrick (1982) demonstrate that if the wealth elasticity of the money demand function is sufficiently high, the excess demand for money can be eliminated by a decline in wealth rather than by appreciation of the exchange rate. The work of Rodriguez (1979) and Mussa (1980) points out that the current account deficit must eventually be paid for by a switch from domestic consumption to the production of exportables which puts downwards pressure on the current exchange rate by implying the necessity of a depreciation in the long run. Considerations of portfolio balance as traced by Branson (1977), Henderson (1979) and Branson and Buiter (1983) imply that expansionary fiscal policy can cause the exchange rate to either appreciate or depreciate depending upon the relative responses of the current and capital accounts of the balance of payments. Greenwood (1983) and Kawai (1985) have generalised this literature by demonstrating how no unique immutable relationship exists between the government's macroeconomic policy mix, interest rates, the exchange rate and the current account of the balance of payments.

Models Based on Optimising Behaviour

The realisation of Lucas (1976) that perceived changes in policy regimes may cause individuals to alter their maximising behaviour in ways which modify many 'postulated' macroeconomic relationships has engendered a sense of urgency into the quest for microfoundations. The significance of this development for the present discussion lies in the fact that a number of recent studies have investigated the operation of fiscal policy in open economies with floating exchange rates using models which are based on individual optimising behaviour. In this vein, Obstfeld (1981), Sachs (1983), Frenkel and Razin (1986) and Cuddington and Vinals (1986a) have constructed Walrasian market-clearing models, while the latter Cuddington and Vinals (1986b) have allowed for the existence of Keynesian unemployment.

Obstfeld (1981) develops an equilibrium model of the determination of the exchange rate and the current account of a small open economy which is inhabited by utility - maximising households with infinite planning horizons who consume a single good and hold only domestic money, although they have access to world credit markets. A tax-financed increase in government expenditure leads to a reduction in private consumption and a depreciation of the exchange rate as domestic residents accumulate net foreign assets in order to finance the higher level of aggregate absorption. This analysis has been extended by Sachs (1983) and by Frenkel and Razin (1986) who investigate the potency of fiscal policy in a general equilibrium, two-country world which is inhabited by overlapping generations of intertemporal utility maximisers. The former researcher illustrates the importance of the wage determination process in predicting the exchange rate effects of fiscal policy initiatives, while the latter researchers demonstrate that the effects depend upon the extent to which the initiative is temporary or permanent in nature and on whether it has been anticipated prior to implementation. Cuddington and Vinals (1986a) allow for the existence of classical and Keynesian unemployment in an economy which is inhabited by intertemporal utility maximisers who consume traded and non-traded goods while forming rational expectations about the effects of current and future policy initiatives of the authorities.

Table 6.1 below provides a summary of the qualitative results which emerge from Mundell-Fleming vintage 'postulated' models when international capital movements are unrestricted across fixed and flexible exchange rates compared with those which emerge from 'optimising' models with Keynesian unemployment. Consider first the effects of a bond financed increase in government expenditure. This raises aggregate demand and imports and causes the current account of the balance of payments to turn into deficit, while the higher interest rates attract inflows of foreign capital which causes the capital account to turn into surplus. With floating exchange rates, the bond financed fiscal expansion will appreciate the foreign exchange value of the domestic currency with the resulting loss in international competitiveness reducing net exports. Under a fixed exchange rate regime, the balance of payments surplus will result in the accumulation of foreign exchange reserves, and in the absence of successful sterilisation behaviour, the money supply will expand. Consider next the effects of expansionary monetary policy. An open market purchase of domestic bonds by the monetary authorities will increase the domestic money supply and cause both the current and capital accounts of the balance of payments to move into deficit. Under a floating exchange rate regime, the monetary expansion will unambiguously depreciate the exchange rate. With fixed exchange rates, the resulting loss of foreign exchange reserves will contract the supply of domestic money unless the authorities can engage in successful sterilisation behaviour. Perhaps the most popular version of the 'optimising' approach is that provided by Cuddington, Johansson and Ohlsson (1985), with Keynesian unemployment and perfect capital mobility. It is constructive to consider the effects of a bond financed fiscal expansion in this model, in which the government raises its demand for non-traded goods. The higher demand for non-tradeables raises aggregate demand via the usual multiplier process which now raises the demand for both traded and non-traded goods and causes the balance of trade to turn to deficit. Under a regime of floating exchange rates, the higher aggregate demand raises the transactions demand for money which necessitates an appreciation of the exchange rate. The effects of an expansionary monetary policy in the model are to reduce domestic interest rates below world rates, which causes an outflow of capital and a depreciation of the exchange rate.

Table 6.1: Postulated and Optimising Open Economy Models with Perfect Capital Mobility

Model Specification	Total output	Output of non-traded goods	Output of traded goods	Exchange rate	Balance of trade
Postulated model					
Fiscal policy					
Fixed Exchange Rate	+			0	–
Flexible Exchange Rate	0			+	–
Monetary policy					
Fixed Exchange Rate	0			0	0
Flexible Exchange Rate	+			–	–
Optimising model					
Fiscal policy					
Fixed Exchange Rate	+	+	0	0	–
Flexible Exchange Rate	?	+	–	+	?
Monetary policy					
Fixed Exchange Rate	0	0	0	0	0
Flexible Exchange Rate	+	+	+	–	?

In summary, the qualitative results which emerge from both types of model are broadly similar when capital movements are unrestricted across fixed exchange rates. This result, however, is not obtained when the authorities operate a floating exchange rate regime. As Kawai (1985) demonstrates, a considerable range of variation can exist depending upon the precise model specification. What perhaps explains the lack of empirical support for the simpler models is that they conceal important complexities in the relationships which exist between the important variables. Kearney (1990) makes this point, and Mizon (1995) points to the econometric modelling implications. In essence, the considerable uncertainty which pervades theoretical modelling of the exchange rate suggests the appropriateness of employing the VAR methodology to examine the impact of fiscal innovations on exchange rates across a multi-country study data set.

Econometric Analysis

The theoretical developments which have been outlined in the previous section point to the importance of the government's financing decision in determining the exchange rate effects of variations in the stance of fiscal policy. The modelling strategy which is adopted in this section explicitly incorporates this factor in the empirical tests. More specifically, the following VAR model is suggested:

$$A(L)Y_t = u_t$$

with;

$$A(L) = I - A_1L - A_2L^2 - ... - A_pL^p$$

$$E(u_t) = 0, E(u,u') = S, \quad E(u_tu_s') = 0 \text{ for } t \neq s,$$

$$E(Y_tu_s') = 0 \text{ for } t \neq s, \text{ and}$$

$$Y_t = (G_t, R_t, M_t, C_t, X_t) \tag{6.1}$$

Equation (6.1) constitutes a standard VAR representation in which Y is a $(1 \times n)$ vector of variables, A is an $(n \times n)$ matrix of coefficients, u is an $(n \times 1)$ vector of white noise disturbances and L denotes the lag operator (ie., $L^iY_t = Y_{t-i}$). The variables which appear in the Y vector are government expenditures (G), tax revenues (R), monetary creation (M), the current account of the balance of payments (C) and the real effective exchange rate (X), which is defined as the domestic price of foreign currency.

The data set consists of quarterly observations on these variables for seven countries (Australia, Britain, Canada, France, Germany, Italy and the US) over the period 1975(2) to 1995(2). The choice of countries in the sample

91

represents the G7 countries with the exception of Japan for which data on tax revenue is not available. These countries were chosen because their currencies represent the 'exchange rate environment'. Furthermore, the addition of these countries to the major focus of the thesis (i.e. Australia) may also be argued from the point that the robustness of the estimation methodology employed in the study may be enhanced by including other countries at similar stages of economic development as Australia. The series have been extracted exclusively from various issues of *International Financial Statistics*. All series (except X) are seasonally adjusted and expressed in nominal terms as a ratio to nominal GDP.

A convenient feature of the VAR system is that it can be estimated by ordinary least squares (OLS) which yields consistent and asymptotically efficient estimates of the A matrix. This situation occurs because the right hand side variables in the VAR model are all predetermined and are the same in each equation. In order to avoid the possibility of obtaining spurious regression estimates, it is first necessary to investigate the stationarity of the data. The stationarity tests were conducted using the Augmented Dickey-Fuller (1979, 1981) and Phillips-Perron (1988) test statistics. The results obtained from running these tests, which are reported in Table 6.2, indicate that although the existence of a unit root cannot be rejected for the levels of the majority of variables at the ten percent level, it is conclusively rejected for the first difference of the variables with the exception of Canada's money and Government expenditure in the Phillips-Perron test and France's Government expenditure and tax revenue. Accordingly, the tests which are reported below are all based on differenced data.

The next step in estimating the model is to decide upon the appropriate lag length (p). In choosing the lag length of a finite-order unrestricted VAR model, one must weigh two opposing considerations: the 'curse of dimensionality' and the correct specification of the model. Since the number of parameters to be estimated quickly increases with the number of lags in the system, models of moderate size can quickly become overparametrized leading to poor and inefficient estimates of the short-run features of the data. Lag lengths that are too short, however, generate statistical models in which only a subset of the existing information is used. The tradeoff between overparameterization and oversimplification is at the heart of almost all statistical selection criteria designed to choose the lag length of VAR models (see for example, Akaike's AIC 1974; Schwertz's 1978 SIC criterion; Sims (1980) maximum likelihood

Table 6.2: Dickey-Fuller and Phillips-Perron Unit Roots Tests for the Variables in the VAR[20]

Country	Variable	Dickey-Fuller Level	Dickey-Fuller First Difference	Phillips-Perron Level	Phillips-Perron First Difference
AUSTRALIA	C	-5.50	-49.60	-3.24	-81.21
	M	1.02	-12.10	1.76	-83.09
	E	0.62	-150.14	0.21	-117.33
	R	-29.40	-238.40	-92.56	-105.56
	X	-0.76	-85.20	-1.50	-83.26
BRITAIN	C	-7.28	-30.74	-12.18	-90.43
	M	0.95	-30.17	1.15	-87.84
	E	0.63	-24.42	0.92	-106.21
	R	0.06	-75.48	-0.92	-95.10
	X	-9.09	-183.95	-5.20	-63.20
CANADA	C	-2.65	-2.65	-10.40	-10.40
	M	-0.21	-5.21	0.32	-0.32
	E	-0.70	-3.70	-0.37	-0.37
	R	-0.44	-6.44	-1.06	-3.06
	X	-10.99	-10.99	-6.93	-6.93
FRANCE	C	-7.44	-184.13	-35.35	-112.94
	M	-1.66	-11.65	-1.37	-131.71
	E	-0.14	22.00	-25.09	-109.62
	R	-0.88	87.00	-1.71	-94.62
	X	-6.90	-29.56	-3.21	-67.97
GERMANY	C	-9.30	-40.32	-15.10	-106.35
	M	1.06	-34.51	1.26	-122.63
	E	0.21	-45.77	-1.38	-68.43
	R	0.28	-34.00	-0.57	-136.74
	X	-10.99	-37.80	-4.68	-73.68
ITALY	C	-2.24	-26.30	-39.62	-48.80
	M	0.66	-10.84	0.32	-82.94
	E	1.13	-23.72	-3.84	-86.03
	R	1.09	-12.00	-7.97	-108.17
	X	-21.82	-25.95	-5.87	-54.43
UNITED STATES	C	-5.30	-29.55	-7.52	-64.87
	M	-0.30	-25.70	0.61	-131.07
	E	-0.00	-23.06	-0.17	-113.86
	R	0.30	-65.11	-3.67	-83.68
	X	0.17	-34.66	0.73	-65.05

ratio (MLR)). In this research, we employ the statistical selection criteria proposed by Hakkio and Morris (1984), which give similar results regardless of whether the testing strategy is from low to high lag orders or the reverse. The results of this procedure are presented in the left hand column of Tables 6.4A - 6.4D where it can be seen that the lag lengths vary between three and four quarters. For congruence, the Breusch-Godfrey residuals-based autocorrelations test, which is presented in the right hand column of Tables 6.4A - 6.4D, provides additional support for this choice of lag length by failing to detect the existence of residual autocorrelation in any of the chosen equations. Significance tests on lagged residuals added to the VAR's variables follow standard distributions even if the variables are unit root processes. In summary, the lag lengths are three for Australia and Canada and four for Britain, France, Germany, Italy and the US. In order to test the parameter constancy of the chosen models, *CHOW* tests for structural stability were conducted for each equation in all countries.   In conducting this test, the sample size was split at the middle. Other choices considered for splitting the data included a 60 percent – 40 percent and 40 percent – 60 percent split in the data, with the results also failing to detect the presence of structural breaks. The results for each country are reported in Table 6.5. The significance levels indicate the lack of any structural break over the period of estimation.

The Estimated VAR Models

Table 6.3 provides a summary description of the performance of the model by presenting the F statistics (with their associated marginal significance levels) of the joint significance of all lags of the relevant variables in each equation of the VAR models. There is evidence of feedback in all countries. More specifically, disregarding the own variable in each equation, the occurrences of feedback are five in Australia, three in Britain and Germany, nine in Canada, four in France and six in Italy and in the US. In what follows, we shall restrict the discussion to the exchange rate equation since this variable is the focus of the analysis. Looking at the exchange rate equation, money financing contributes significantly at the five percent level in Canada, tax revenue contributes significantly to the determination of the exchange rate in Canada and Germany, and government expenditure contributes significantly at the five percent level in the US. Table 6.3 also demonstrates the existence of significant feedback effects from the exchange rate to the other variables in the VAR models. For example, the exchange rate contributes significantly to the determination of tax revenues at the five percent level in the US, to government expenditure in Australia, and to monetary financing in Canada.

An interesting finding which also emerges from inspection of Table 6.3 concerns the 'twin deficits' hypothesis according to which variations in the

Table 6.3: Significance Tests for Inclusion of All Lags of Variables

Equation	Australia	Britain	Canada	France	Germany	Italy	USA
(1) Government Expenditure							
ΔG	49.66 (0.00)*	1.05 (0.40)	8.5 (0.00)*	24.68 (0.00)*	5.43 (0.00)*	3.26 (0.02)*	15.18 (0.00)*
ΔR	2.54 (0.05)*	2.59 (0.05)*	5.7 (0.00)*	1.62 (0.18)	1.21 (0.31)	5.33 (0.00)*	1.32 (0.27)
ΔM	2.65 (0.05)*	0.83 (0.50)	5.18 (0.00)*	3.30 (0.02)*	2.02 (0.10)	6.82 (0.00)*	1.73 (0.15)
ΔC	1.95 (0.13)	1.51 (0.21)	4.81 (0.00)*	1.12 (0.35)	2.11 (0.09)	1.68 (0.17)	1.18 (0.33)
ΔX	2.53 (0.05)*	0.98 (0.42)	1.50 (0.22)	0.15 (0.48)	0.43 (.078)	0.70 (0.60)	0.85 (0.50)
(2) Tax Receipts							
ΔG	0.17 (0.91)	1.71 (0.16)	1.3 (0.26)	2.57 (0.04)*	0.64 (0.63)	2.83 (0.03)*	3.11 (0.02)*
ΔR	19.6 (0.00)*	37.28 (0.00)*	5.3 (0.00)*	8.09 (0.00)*	12.80 (0.00)*	19.20 (0.00)*	67.00 (0.00)*
ΔM	0.19 (0.90)	1.36 (0.25)	1.37 (0.26)	1.77 (0.15)	0.32 (0.86)	2.12 (0.09)	5.61 (0.00)*
ΔC	2.63 (0.05)*	1.47 (0.22)	0.26 (0.85)	0.97 (0.42)	5.43 (0.00)*	1.40 (0.25)	1.21 (0.32)
ΔX	0.32 (0.80)	0.87 (0.98)	0.90 (0.44)	0.89 (0.47)	1.77 (0.15)	1.05 (0.40)	5.48 (0.00)*
(3) Monetary Financing							
ΔG	1.55 (0.21)	0.19 (0.93)	2.8 (0.04)*	3.08 (0.03)*	1.67 (0.17)	3.43 (0.00)*	2.07 (0.09)
ΔR	0.88 (0.45)	0.92 (0.45)	2.7 (0.05)*	2.00 (0.10)	1.50 (0.20)	4.75 (0.00)*	3.02 (0.02)*
ΔM	0.31 (0.11)	0.36 (0.83)	3.27 (0.02)*	5.23 (0.00)*	5.0 (0.00)*	8.20 (0.00)*	1.77 (0.14)
ΔC	2.00 (0.12)	0.49 (0.73)	1.93 (0.13)	1.63 (0.18)	0.40 (0.81)	4.68 (0.00)*	0.53 (0.71)
ΔX	2.04 (0.11)	0.97 (0.43)	3.50 (0.02)*	0.50 (0.73)	0.83 (0.51)	1.99 (0.11)	2.21 (0.08)
(4) Current Account							
ΔG	2.5 (0.07)	0.10 (0.65)	2.66 (0.05)*	1.36 (0.25)	0.28 (0.88)	0.60 (0.65)	2.04 (0.10)
ΔR	0.24 (0.86)	0.67 (0.01)*	0.08 (0.96)	2.57 (0.04)*	0.43 (0.78)	1.65 (0.18)	7.4 (0.00)*
ΔM	4.70 (0.00)*	0.06 (0.03)*	1.12 (0.34)	0.60 (0.66)	3.15 (0.02)*	1.52 (0.30)	1.97 (0.11)
ΔC	1.7 (0.17)	0.07 (0.83)	4.70 (0.00)*	7.8 (0.00)*	6.40 (0.00)*	2.37 (0.07)	3.40 (0.01)*
ΔX	1.63 (0.19)	2951 (0.50)	0.30 (0.82)	1.07 (0.37)	0.22 (0.92)	0.09 (0.98)	1.90 (0.12)
(5) Exchange Rate							
ΔG	1.34 (0.09)	0.42 (0.78)	1.88 (0.14)	1.40 (0.24)	0.17 (0.95)	1.67 (0.15)	2.80 (0.03)*
ΔR	0.34 (0.80)	0.54 (0.70)	5.52 (0.00)*	1.03 (0.40)	2.5 (0.05)*	0.78 (0.54)	0.66 (0.62)
ΔM	2.37 (0.07)	0.73 (0.57)	6.14 (0.00)*	0.80 (0.53)	0.06 (0.99)	1.92 (0.13)	0.72 (0.58)
ΔC	0.41 (0.75)	0.97 (0.42)	0.17 (0.91)	0.21 (0.92)	1.45 (0.23)	0.70 (0.60)	2.21 (0.08)
ΔX	0.61 (0.60)	1.03 (0.40)	3.81 (0.01)*	1.05 (0.38)	0.53 (0.71)	1.65 (0.18)	2.02 (0.10)

Table 6.4A: Sum of Coefficients Tax Revenue Equation

	Lag Length	Constant	ΔG	ΔR	ΔM	ΔC	ΔX	R2	Breusch-Godfrey	Q
Australia	3	43.27 (0.94)	0.37 (0.74)	-1.9 (0.00)	0.03 (0.92)	2.75 (0.01)	-660.82 (0.94)	0.45	2.41 (0.65)	11.64 (0.82)
Britain	4	1122 (0.02)	-0.24 (0.58)	-0.75 (0.11)	0.09 (0.06)	0.24 (0.68)	12257 (0.13)	0.86	2.74 (0.60)	17.15 (0.44)
Canada	3	1.03 (0.04)	-0.57 (0.31)	-1.55 (0.00)	0.16 (0.44)	0.19 (0.62)	-26.82 (0.14)	0.63	6.98 (0.13)	8.33 (0.95)
France	4	8.00 (0.03)	-0.48 (0.10)	-2.11 (0.00)	0.39 (0.01)	-0.80 (0.25)	4.00 (0.31)	0.76	7.42 (0.11)	16.65 (0.47)
Germany	4	0.98 (0.25)	0.46 (0.23)	-1.05 (0.03)	0.09 (0.31)	-0.34 (0.22)	19.80 (0.12)	0.80	5.54 (0.23)	24.8 (0.09)
Italy	4	2207 (0.37)	-0.10 (0.85)	-0.52 (0.30)	0.20 (0.60)	-0.90 (0.36)	-1297 (0.88)	0.97	5.03 (0.28)	14.00 (0.67)
USA	4	-275 (0.92)	1.92 (0.00)	-3.20 (0.00)	0.46 (0.31)	-0.22 (0.85)	-25349 (0.15)	0.95	2.63 (0.62)	17.40 (0.42)

Table 6.4B: Sum of Coefficients Government Expenditure Equation

	Lag Length	Constant	ΔG	ΔR	ΔM	ΔC	ΔX	R2	Breusch-Godfrey	Q
Australia	3	990.36 (0.00)	-1.93 (0.00)	-0.13 (0.13)	0.00 (0.92)	0.26 (0.29)	6530.82 (0.05)	0.75	3.52 (0.47)	17.33 (0.43)
Britain	4	1251 (0.00)	-0.46 (0.20)	-0.16 (0.67)	0.03 (0.73)	0.49 (0.32)	4041 (0.55)	0.48	4.80 (0.30)	20.9 (0.23)
Canada	3	1.41 (0.00)	-1.44 (0.00)	-0.09 (0.68)	-0.18 (0.11)	0.58 (0.01)	-18.43 (0.08)	0.74	7.19 (0.12)	34.51 (0.00)
France	4	14.38 (0.04)	-2.01 (0.00)	0.76 (0.41)	-0.09 (0.72)	-1.72 (0.21)	7.60 (0.92)	0.95	7.73 (0.10)	20.00 (0.24)
Germany	4	1.20 (0.27)	-0.74 (0.14)	-0.73 (0.24)	0.21 (0.08)	-0.31 (0.40)	-5.80 (0.72)	0.72	2.66 (0.61)	16.16 (0.51)
Italy	4	2207 (0.37)	-0.10 (0.85)	-0.52 (0.29)	0.20 (0.60)	-0.91 (0.36)	-1291 (0.88)	0.97	5.03 (0.28)	13.90 (0.67)
USA	4	16.25 (0.00)	-2.18 (0.00)	-0.40 (0.47)	-0.41 (0.67)	0.92 (0.12)	-114.11 (0.08)	0.72	5.68 (0.22)	9.3 (0.92)

Table 6.4C: Sum of Coefficients Monetary Financing Equation

	Lag Length	Constant	ΔG	ΔR	ΔM	ΔC	ΔX	R2	Breusch-Godfrey	Q
Australia	3	734.31 (0.02)	-0.43 (0.43)	0.28 (0.11)	0.31 (0.11)	-0.40 (0.46)	4300.4 (0.54)	0.23	8.04 (0.09)	20.67 (0.24)
Britain	4	3064 (0.23)	-1.13 (0.61)	1.25 (0.60)	0.16 (0.53)	-1.57 (0.61)	-3256 (0.44)	0.24	5.01 (0.28)	6.77 (0.98)
Canada	3	-0.24 (0.65)	1.19 (0.06)	0.70 (0.12)	0.48 (0.03)	-1.03 (0.02)	38.26 (0.06)	0.64	7.19 (0.12)	22.42 (0.16)
France	4	1.81 (0.76)	-0.08 (0.85)	1.17 (0.16)	0.58 (0.02)	2.90 (0.02)	70.37 (0.32)	0.86	8.00 (0.90)	6.50 (0.10)
Germany	4	4.35 (0.13)	0.63 (0.62)	-1.20 (0.46)	0.48 (0.13)	0.54 (0.55)	-70.8 (0.10)	0.80	6.81 (0.14)	13.20 (0.72)
Italy	4	4951 (0.05)	0.77 (1.31)	-0.11 (0.80)	0.09 (0.80)	1.02 (0.34)	-4448 (0.78)	0.95	1.81 (0.76)	13.20 (0.70)
USA	4	21.32 (0.22)	-1.63 (0.04)	-1.96 (0.04)	0.36 (0.23)	0.65 (0.51)	-45.24 (0.70)	0.80	5.52 (0.23)	10.25 (0.64)

Table 6.4D: Sum of Coefficients Exchange Rate

	Lag Length	Constant	ΔG	ΔR	ΔM	ΔC	ΔX	R2	Breusch-Godfrey	Q
Australia	3	0.01 (0.30)	-0.00 (0.70)	-0.00 (0.40)	-0.00 (0.41)	-0.00 (0.51)	-0.16 (0.55)	0.10	6.12 (0.18)	24.4 (0.10)
Britain	4	7.00 (0.63)	0.00 (0.60)	0.00 (0.73)	-0.00 (0.29)	-0.00 (0.40)	0.07 (0.27)	0.17	8.81 (0.06)	17.23 (0.43)
Canada	3	0.01 (0.02)	-0.00 (0.21)	-0.00 (0.22)	-0.00 (0.03)	-0.00 (0.92)	0.13 (0.54)	0.24	7.45 (0.11)	20.75 (0.23)
France	4	-0.00 (0.89)	0.00 (0.27)	-0.11 (0.94)	-0.00 (0.48)	-0.02 (0.54)	0.30 (0.17)	0.27	3.51 (0.47)	23.35 (0.13)
Germany	4	0.00 (0.59)	0.00 (0.99)	-0.00 (0.22)	0.00 (0.91)	-0.00 (0.42)	0.31 (0.18)	0.02	2.66 (0.61)	19.37 (0.30)
Italy	4	-0.31 (0.45)	-0.00 (0.28)	-0.00 (0.12)	0.00 (0.09)	0.00 (0.94)	0.20 (0.70)	0.02	7.37 (0.11)	6.61 (0.98)
USA	4	-0.00 (0.54)	0.00 (0.22)	0.00 (0.87)	0.00 (0.77)	-0.00 (0.04)	0.50 (0.04)	0.15	5.58 (0.23)	7.03 (0.98)

stance of fiscal policy tend to be associated with corresponding variations in the economy's current account balance. The Table presents little evidence for this hypothesis. Rather, consistent with the findings of Kearney and Monadjemi (1990), the existence of significant feedback effects from the current account balance to fiscal policy variables does not support the view of fiscal policy as the control variable which 'causes' current account performance.

Table 6.4 sheds further light upon the issues raised above by presenting the sums of lag coefficients for each of the explanatory variables in the equations of the VAR model. These tables are useful because the individual coefficient estimates of the A-matrix in equation (1) do not convey much information, and because they provide a sound intuition for interpreting the models' impulse response functions. Examination of the diagnostics in the last two columns of the Tables confirms that the model is well specified with no evidence of residual autocorrelation.

Of particular interest in the context of this research is the finding in Table 6.4(D) of a negative relationship between the exchange rate and the level of government expenditure in only three (Australia, Canada and Italy) of the seven countries, although it is not statistically significant. Examination of the reverse relationship between the level of government expenditure and the exchange rate in Table 6.4B suggests a negative relationship in four countries which is statistically significant at the ten percent level in Canada and the US. The remaining countries indicate a positive relationship which issignificant at the five percent level only in the case of Australia. As emphasised previously, however, the government's financing decision is important in assessing the overall effects of variations in the stance of fiscal policy, and the results in these tables corroborate those of Table 6.3 in detecting a considerable degree of reverse causation in all countries studied. It is with considerable interest, therefore, that we now turn to consider the impulse response functions in order to discern the extent to which our international data set provides non-ambiguous results about how fiscal policy innovations together with the government's financing decision impinges on the exchange rate.

The Impulse Response Functions

The primary advantage of the VAR approach is that it allows us to capture general dynamic regularities in the data without imposing possibly invalid identifying restrictions. Interpretations of the VARS are based on the vector moving average (VMA) representation in which each variable is expressed as a linear combination of its own current innovation and lagged innovations of all the variables in the system. If there is no contemporaneous correlation among the innovations, it is possible to uniquely decompose the variance of each variable into components accounted for by each innovation. In general, however, the innovations are contemporaneously correlated and so a unique decomposition does not exist. To resolve the problem one applies a triangular orthogonalizing transformation to the vector of innovations in order to obtain a new vector of "orthogonalized innovations" which are contemporaneously uncorrelated. The transformation is not unique and by selecting one, the user arbitrarily imposes a particular causal ordering on the variables in the VAR model. The variance decomposition (VDC) of each variable in the system summarizes the information contained in the VMA representation. The VDC measures the contribution of each innovation in the VAR to the k-step ahead forecast error variance of the dependent variables. It is a useful tool for determining the relative quantative importance of shocks to the variables in the system. The IRFs reported in the paper are, therefore, based on the orthogonalisation of the errors by ordering the variables in the Y vector according to their influence on the other variables in the system.

Table 6.6 provides the results of this exercise for each of the seven countries. A number of observations emerge which are relevant to the interpretation of the IRFs. *First*, no variable is completely exogenous insofar as less than a 100 percent of the 40-step ahead prediction of each variable is explained by innovations in itself. At a maximum, 80 percent of the 40-step ahead prediction error of any variable that is explained by innovations in itself appears in three cases, that of revenue (R) and the exchange rate (X) in Australia, and money (M) in the US. *Second*, the ranking of variables by degree of exogeneity is different in each country. For example, tax revenue (R) ranks from being the most exogenous to the least exogenous variable (in Australia and Italy respectively). This variation reflects different market and political structures and institutions which partly explains why the simply specified theoretical models fail many empirical applications while also explaining why different countries react differently to similar economic disturbances. Having appropriately orthogonalised the errors in equation (1), we will now examine the IRFs.

In order to appropriately model the fiscal financing decisions, we first write the government budget constraint as:

$$G = R + \Delta B + \Delta M \qquad (6.2)$$

where symbols retain their prior meaning, B is the outstanding stock of government debt and Δ denotes the change in a variable. Equation (6.2) thus states that the fiscal deficit (G-R) can be financed by issuing debt (Δ B) or by expanding the money supply (Δ M). Figures 6.1 - 6.3 depict the IRFs for the exchange rate to the following fiscal policy innovations:

- an increase in government expenditure which is financed by issuing debt (i.e. bond financing with G = Δ B);

- an increase in government expenditure which is financed by raising taxes (i.e. a balanced budget fiscal expansion) with $G = R$
- Ricardian equivalence a swap of taxes for debt (with $- R = \Delta B$).

In each case, an innovation of one standard deviation in the relevant variable has been normalised to unity in order to ensure that the budget constraint in (6.2) applies to the innovations. Simulation (6.1) was performed by noting that a fiscal expansion which is not financed by raising taxes or by monetary expansion must be financed residually by issuing more debt. Simulation (6.2) was conducted by impulsing both government spending and tax revenues by the same sized innovation. Simulation (6.3) was conducted by reducing taxes alone. All variables continue to be expressed as a ratio to nominal GDP in order to facilitate international comparison of the IRFs. The Figures present the IRFs of the response of the exchange rate to the various shocks.

Firstly, consider Simulation (1), which gives the response of the exchange rate to the bond financed fiscal expansion. Perhaps the most obvious conclusion which emerges from casual inspection of the Figure concerns the richness of the adjustment dynamics. The exchange rate (defined as the domestic price of a unit of foreign currency) initially appreciates in three countries (Australia, Italy and the US), while it depreciates in the other four countries (Britain, Canada, France and Germany). It then experiences sustained weakness in five countries (Australia, Britain, Canada, Italy and the US) which is unwound after approximately 12 quarters before settling down to its original level. These results are intuitive in the light of the sums of coefficients which are presented in Table 6.4 insofar as the sums of coefficients for the government spending variable in the exchange rate equation were found to be positive in four of the seven countries studied (Britain, France, Germany and the US) and negative in the remaining three countries (Australia, Canada and Italy). Consider next Simulation (2) which gives the response of the exchange rate to the tax financed fiscal expansion. This corresponds to the so-called 'balanced budget' case insofar as the innovation to the tax revenues is of the same magnitude as the innovation to the level of government spending. The results in this case are somewhat less ambiguous as might be expected. The exchange rate initially appreciates in five of the seven countries (Australia, France, Germany, Italy and the US) and depreciates in two of the remaining countries studied (Canada and the Britain). Once again, these results are in general accord with those of Table 6.4 (B) where it can be seen that the sum of the coefficients of the government spending and tax variables are negative in the countries where this innovation appreciates the exchange rate (apart from the US).

Finally, Simulation (3) depicts the response of the exchange rate to a swap of taxes for debt with no change in the level of government spending. As

100

Table 6.5: Chow Test

Country	ΔC		ΔM		ΔE		ΔR		ΔX	
Australia	1.59	(0.19)	0.82	(0.48)	1.76	(0.16)	1.65	(0.18)	0.67	(0.56)
Britain	1.72	(0.17)	0.34	(0.79)	1.81	(0.15)	1.72	(0.17)	2.59	(0.06)
Canada	2.39	(0.07)	2.53	(0.06)	2.69	(0.06)	1.76	(0.16)	0.89	(0.40)
France	2.88	(0.01)	0.85	(0.46)	2.52	(0.06)	0.59	(0.62)	3.58	(0.01)
Germany	2.48	(0.06)	0.17	(0.91)	1.31	(0.27)	0.76	(0.51)	1.51	(0.21)
Italy	1.26	(0.29)	1.73	(0.17)	2.54	(0.06)	3.13	(0.03)	2.67	(0.06)
US	0.90	(0.44)	1.92	(0.13)	1.59	(0.20)	1.01	(0.39)	2.58	(0.06)

Table 6.6: Variance of Decomposition of the VAR Systems

Country	Percentage of 40-step Ahead Prediction Error in Y Which is Explained by Innovations in (G R M C X)				
	ΔG	ΔR	ΔM	ΔC	ΔX
Australia	66.87	92.11	49.97	53.62	81.20
Britain	41.30	55.88	77.14	47.22	70.00
Canada	39.88	37.06	52.13	58.25	43.33
France	56.50	28.13	26.66	70.00	56.64
Germany	29.18	39.20	46.66	68.10	53.60
Italy	22.00	0.20	37.00	42.70	00.30
US	47.88	16.52	81.86	45.31	58.02

with the previous simulation, the results are not uniform across countries. The exchange rate initially depreciates in four countries (Australia, Britain, Canada and Italy) and appreciates in the remaining three (France, Germany and the US). It is noteworthy in this case that the adjustment path is generally shorter than in the other simulations. Both the 'postulated' and 'optimising' macromodels examined suggest that under a flexible exchange rate regime with perfect capital mobility, the exchange rate response to an expansionary (contractionary) fiscal policy causes the exchange rate to appreciate (depreciate). Simulation (1) shows the impulse responses to this fiscal innovation, where three out of the seven countries initially show an appreciation in their exchange rates. Exchange rate responses are therefore not uniform across countries to this variant of fiscal innovation. The IRFs in Simulation (2) for a tax financed balanced budget fiscal expansion show an initial appreciation in the exchange rate for five of the seven countries studied. Three of these countries Australia, Italy and the US also experience an exchange rate appreciation in the case of a debt financed fiscal expansion, which suggests that for these countries the exchange rate moves in the same direction regardless of the method of financing. This finding supports evidence that shows tax financed and debt financed fiscal expansions are equivalent, (see *inter alia* Aschauer (1985); Feldstein (1986); and Gruen (1988)). Finally, the exchange rate response to reducing taxes alone causes an appreciation in three of the seven countries studied. This evidence supports both of the models outcomes examined in Table 6.1 above, which would indicate that a expansionary fiscal policy (reduce taxes) causes the exchange rate to appreciate. This also provides international evidence which support the findings of Plosser (1982).

Summary and Conclusions

Theoretical open economy macroeconomic models of recent vintage yield divergent predictions about how variations in the stance of fiscal policy and in the method of its financing impinge upon the exchange rate. In view of the considerable uncertainty which pervades appropriate specification of these macromodels, the empirical analysis of this chapter adopted the VAR approach which constitutes an unrestricted reduced form of some unknown structural model. Using quarterly data over the period 1975(2) - 1995(2), models were estimated for seven countries (Australia, Britain, Canada, France, Germany, Italy and the US) in order to examine the extent to which variations in fiscal financing decisions impinge upon the exchange rate.

Amongst our main findings are: *first,* a bond financed fiscal expansion initially appreciates the exchange rate in three countries (Australia, Italy and the US) while a depreciation occurs in the other four countries (Britain, Canada,

Figure 6.1: The Exchange Rate Effects of an Unanticipated Bond Financed Increase in Government Expenditure

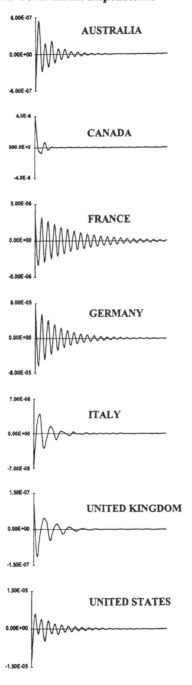

Figure 6.2: The Exchange Rate Effects of an Unanticipated Balanced Budget Increase in Government Expenditure

Figure 6.3: The Exchange Rate Effects of an Unanticipated Money Financed Increase in Government Expenditure

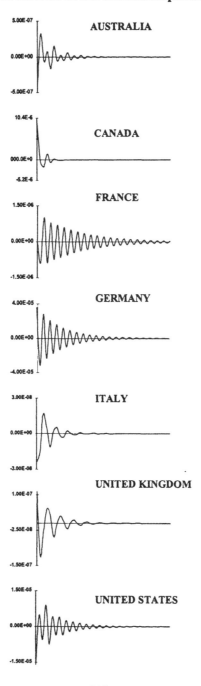

France and Germany); *second*, the exchange rate response to a tax financed fiscal expansion causes an initial appreciation in five of the seven countries studied (Australia, France, Germany, Italy and the US) while a depreciation occurs in the remaining two countries studies (Britain and Canada); *third*, the response of the exchange rate for a swap of taxes for debt with no change in the level of government expenditure, causes the exchange rate to appreciate in three countries (France, Germany and the US) and depreciate in the remaining four (Australia, Britain, Canada and Italy). In conclusion, although the findings reported in this chapter provide some international evidence in favour of the Ricardian view of budget deficits in open economies, the overall conclusion is reached that no consistent pattern can be found in the exchange rate response to fiscal financing decisions.

7 The Effects of Exchange Rate Volatility on the Volume of Japan's Bi-lateral Trade

Introduction

The evidence from the previous chapter indicates that the more volatile exchange rate environment since the introduction of floating exchange rates in the early 1970s appears to be associated with the conduct of government fiscal financing decisions. To maintain the focus of the thesis, this chapter develops and estimates empirical models which examine the effects of exchange rate volatility on international trade flows. Many economists have expressed concern that this rise in exchange rate volatility has reduced the allocational efficiency of the international monetary system. An important ingredient of this concern has been the extent to which the volume of international trade flows has been impeded. This issue possesses important welfare and policy implications, and it has consequently given birth to an increasingly voluminous theoretical and empirical literature.

The important theoretical developments by, *inter alia*, Clark (1973), Ethier (1973), Hooper and Kohlhagen (1978) and Cushman (1983, 1986) have provided useful insights into the ways in which exchange rate volatility may impede international trade flows. The empirical studies, however, have failed to provide unambiguous evidence in favor of the theoretical predictions. The IMF (1984) survey of the effects of exchange rate variability on world trade concludes that: "The large majority of empirical studies on the impact of exchange rate variability on the volume of international trade are unable to establish a systematically significant link between measured exchange rate variability and the volume of international trade, whether on an aggregate or on a bilateral basis" (IMF (1984), pp. 27). For example, Makin (1976), Hooper and Kohlhagen (1978), Gotur (1985) and Bailey, Tavlas and Ulan (1986, 1987) were unable to find statistically significant negative effects of exchange rate volatility on trade flows, while Cushman (1983, 1986) found some such effects and Akhtar and Hilton (1984), Kenen and Rodrick (1986) and Kumar and Dhawan (1991) found stronger effects. It is interesting to note that, in several of the above studies, a significant positive effect of exchange rate volatility on the volume of trade appears. Although theoretical work has generally indicated that exchange rate risk should reduce international trade flows, the empirical studies have provided ambiguous results.

Theoretical considerations have traditionally been unambiguous in suggesting that increased uncertainty should reduce the level of trade. However, recent work by Dellas and Zilberfarb (1989) and Viaene (1992) have provided a theoretical basis for a positive effect of exchange rate variability on trade. Dellas and Zilberfarb (1989) model nominal unhedged trade contracts as standard risky assets that can be analyzed in a conventional asset portfolio framework. Within this framework the trade effects of an increase in exchange rate volatility will, in general, depend on the risk aversion parameter of the model. They indicate that existing work on the effects of exchange rate uncertainty on trade has employed a restrictive version of the portfolio choice model which leads to an unambiguously negative relationship. Giovannini[21] (1988) discusses the case where increases in exchange rate volatility do not necessarily lead firms to restrict supply, and where, if export prices are invoiced in domestic currency, expected profits might actually increase as a result of increased exchange rate risk, leading firms to reduce their export prices. Klein's (1990) study examined the effects of real exchange rate volatility on specific categories of bilateral exports from the US over the period 1978 to 1986, from which he concludes that real exchange rate volatility may stimulate export supply by risk neutral-firms through its effects on their expected profits.

This chapter argues that prior empirical work on the relationship between international trade flows and exchange rate volatility employing time series data is flawed in three important respects. *First*, previous researchers have failed to notice that the volatility variables are generally integrated of orders different from the variables in the trade flow equations. This potentially introduces spurious regression problems and biases the estimated coefficients on the volatility variables towards zero. *Second*, previous empirical work has not followed a consistent modeling strategy in capturing the dynamics of the trade volume equations. This problem is overcome in the present analysis by implementing the general-to-specific estimation methodology of Hendry (1974, 1977), Hendry and Mizon (1977) and Davidson et al (1978). *Finally*, the testing methodology adopted here lies in contrast to the sought for negative coefficient in prior empirical work by testing the null hypothesis of zero volatility effect against the correct alternative hypothesis of a non-zero volatility effect.

The chapter is organized as follows. The chapter begins with an outline of the theoretical framework. Next, an empirical analysis is presented based upon a consistent set of industry-specific bilateral trade volume and price data for eight countries (Australia, Britain, Canada, France, Germany, Italy, Japan and the US) over the period 1978(1) - 1992(2). Finally, a summary of the main findings are discussed with the chapter concluding that exchange rate volatility is at least as likely to raise trade flows as it is to impede them.

Theoretical Framework

The theoretical basis for the empirical analysis reported in this paper follows in the tradition of Cushman's (1983, 1986) and Klein's (1990) modification of the Hooper-Kohlhagen (1978) supply and demand model. The features of the model are, firstly, that foreign exchange uncertainty is assumed to be the only source of risk for traders in the economy. This is achieved by deflating the monetary variables appearing in the model at the same rate within countries, leaving the firm to face uncertainty only about changes in the real exchange rate. Secondly, the firm's utility depends on real profits `a la` Cushman (1983, 1986) rather than on nominal profits as in Hooper and Kohlhagen (1978), with all variables specified in real terms with respect to their own price level.[22] Thirdly, firms expect country-specific wages and prices to grow at one common inflation rate so that intra-country relative price volatility can be excluded from the analysis in order to focus on inter-country real exchange rate variability. The real exchange rate S is defined as the domestic currency price of one unit of the importing country's currency multiplied by the ratio of the foreign to the domestic price level. If S rises, future trade appears relatively more profitable to exporters so export supply will vary directly with changes in S. To capture the impact of exchange rate volatility on a country's exports, we follow the practice of Cushman (1983) and Kenen and Rodrik (1986) in measuring exchange rate risk by taking the absolute value of the four quarter moving standard deviation of the quarterly percentage change in the bilateral real exchange rate between the exporting country and the importing country.[23] It is worth noting that there are some limitations to the use of the four quarter moving standard deviation as a measure for exchange rate volatility, in that this measure may underestimate the actual cost of exchange rate changes by smoothing the movements, and in the degree of arbitrariness of deciding on the number of quarters over which to estimate the model. Several investigations in this area have, however, used a moving average of the standard deviation of the exchange rate as a proxy for exchange rate volatility,[24] and this procedure is accordingly adopted in the current analysis. The following reduced form export quantity equation, with expected signs, provides the framework for the more detailed specification which is outlined in the empirical section of the paper:

$$Q_{ik} = E(Y_k, C_k, W_i, W_k, S_{ik}, V_{ik})$$

$$E'_1 > 0, \ E'_2 < 0, \ E'_3 < 0, \ E'_4 < 0, \ E'_5 > 0, \ E'_6 \overset{>}{<} 0. \qquad (7.1)$$

Here, Q_{ik} denotes the volume of exports from country i to k, Y_k denotes real GNP in the importing country, C_k is the importer's non-price rationing, (measured by capacity utilisation in the importing country), Wi and W_k are the real unit labour costs of the exporters and importers respectively, S is the real exchange rate and V is the volatility of the real exchange rate.

Exchange Rate Volatility and the Volume of Exports

The period of estimation spans the floating exchange rate period from 1978(1) to 1992(2). This avoids Kenen and Rodrik's (1986) objection to combining the fixed and the floating periods due to a change in structure. A regression equation which captures the impact of exchange rate volatility on the volume of bilateral exports from country i to country k can be presented as follows:

$$Q_{ik} = a_0 + a_1 Y_k + a_2 C_k + a_3 W_i + a_4 W_k + a_5 S_{ik} + a_6 V_{ik}$$

$$+ a_7 Q_{ik} + e_t \quad a_1 > 0, \ a_2 < 0, \ a_3 < 0, \ a_4 < 0, \ a_5 > 0, \ a_6 \overset{>}{<} 0 \qquad (7.2)$$

The formulation of proxies for each of these independent variables follows theoretical convention. The real income variable[25] for each country was proxied by seasonally adjusted gross national product (GNP). According to theory, income in trading-partner countries should contribute to the determination of a nation's exports, and since the marginal propensity to import with respect to income is positive, the expected sign on a nation's trading partners' income, Y_k, should also be positive. Importer's capacity utilisation, C_k, acts as a price variable in the equation. As demand pressure and capacity utilisation rise during cyclical upswings, available supply is rationed through such techniques as longer order delivery lags and tighter customer credit conditions, thereby depressing quantity demanded. In theory, an increase in the importing firm's nonprice rationing would depress domestic demand and hence import quantity demanded, so the expected sign is negative. With respect to real unit labour costs, a rise in the importers unit labour costs, W_k, leads to a decrease in domestic supply and therefore in the derived demand for imports. We therefore expect there to be an negative relationship between W_k and the volume of exports to that country Q_{ik}. Equally plausible however, is that an increase in unit labour costs of the exporter, W_i, will reduce exports from country i to k. If the real exchange rate, S, rises, future trade appears relatively more profitable to exporters, so export supply will vary directly with changes in S. The effect of exchange rate volatility V on exports is indeterminate. The reasons for this indeterminacy are important in the current context. If firms are risk averse, exchange rate volatility operates as a negative supply shock which shifts the supply schedule backwards and raises export prices while reducing volumes. As Giovannini (1988) demonstrates, a risk-neutral firm with export prices invoiced in domestic currency may cut prices in response to exchange rate volatility. In this case, an increase in exchange rate volatility is associated with a positive/negative effect on trade flows, insofar as an elastic (inelastic) demand schedule is associated with an increase (decrease) in trade flows. The overall effect of exchange rate volatility on trade volume depends on firms attitude towards risk, but it also depends on the price elasticity of demand for the firms exports.

The empirical analysis uses a multi-country dataset of Japan's bilateral industry-specific trade flows with its seven major trading partners (Australia, Britain, Canada, France, Germany, Italy, and the US) together with other fundamental economic data on activity, costs, prices and exchange rates which feature in the theoretical framework. These countries were chosen because their currencies represent the 'exchange rate environment'. Also Japan's bilateral trade with the seven countries in this study represents approximately 42 percent of all Japan's trade over the period of this study, while the combined volume of bilateral trade for the industrial countries apart from the US is as large as the US's bilateral trade flows with Japan. The data are sampled quarterly over the period 1978:1 - 1992:2 which covers the post Bretton-Woods regime of floating exchange rates. Details of the construction of variables along with data sources are provided in the Data Appendix.

The Effects of Exchange Rate Volatility on Trade

The testing strategy begins by examining the order of integration of all variables used in the analysis. The unit root tests used here replicate those detailed by Dolado and Jenkinson (1987) which are based upon the exact null and alternative hypotheses under which Dickey (1976), Fuller (1976) and Dickey and Fuller (1979, 1981), constructed the critical values for their DF and ADF test statistics. Table 7.1 table presents this sequential testing procedure based on the augmented Dickey-Fuller tests for the levels, and first differences of Japan's bilateral trade flow variables with its major trading partners. With the exception of Canada's imports, the augmented Dickey-Fuller statistics are greater than their critical values, while the first differences appear stationary with the unit root hypothesis being clearly rejected. Japan's export and import volumes are therefore I(1) with the exception of imports from Canada which appears as I(0). The unit root tests pertaining to the other variables (not reported here, but available on request) indicate that real economic activity (Y) variables are generally I(1) with the exception of Australia which is I(0). With regard to the capacity utilisation series (C), six of the seven countries are I(1), the exception being the US which appears as I(0). Real exchange rate variables (S) are all I(1). The exchange rate variability terms (V) are all I(0) as expected. This is an important finding since, as alluded to previously, prior empirical work has failed to account for the econometric implications of this fact.

The trade volume equations to be estimated therefore take the form:

$$\Delta^d Q_{ik} = a_0 + a_1 \Delta^d Y_k + a_2 \Delta^d C_k + a_3 \Delta^d W_i + a_4 \Delta^d W_k$$

$$+ a_5 \Delta^d S_{ik} + a_6 \Delta^d V_{ik} + a_7 \Delta^d Q_{ik} + e_t \qquad (7.3)$$

There symbols retain their prior meanings, expected signs are as in equation (7.2) and the Δ^d term denotes that a variable is integrated of order d, so that the variable appears differenced d times in the regression equations. Since this chapter's aim is to contribute to the relevant literature by improving upon the dynamic modelling of the relationship between exchange rate volatility and trade flows, it is interesting to investigate the possibility of uncovering useful cointegrating relationships which could form the basis of estimating an error correction model (ECM). If such cointegrating relationships exist, the dynamics can be specified in a manner which constrains the short run relationships to be consistent with their long run counterparts. The unit root test results indicate, however, that useful cointegrating relationships between the variables relevant to this study can not be found. More specifically, the only potentially useful long run relationship which could emerge in this analysis is between the volatility of the real exchange rate variables, V_{ik}, and the trade flow variables, Q_{ik}. However, for there to be a cointegrating relationship between these variables, each series should be integrated of the same order. The results from the unit root tests, however, indicate that they are integrated of different orders. This rules out the existence of a useful ECM representation of the data generation process in the current research.

Empirical Results

The equations are estimated for each country in the study over the period 1978(1) - 1992(2) with up to four (4) lags on each variable. The resulting equations are subsequently restricted using the general-to-specific methodology of Hendry (1974, 1977), Hendry and Mizon (1977) and Davidson et al (1978) until the results in Tables 7.2 and 7.3 are obtained. Previous tests have typically involved regressing trade volumes on variables that may influence demand and supply of traded goods without specifying how the lag structure (if any) was chosen. The tables are interpretable by noting that Table 7.2 reports the results for the trade flows from Japan to the other countries in the sample, while Table 7.3 reports the reciprocal trade flows from these countries to Japan. Concerning the equations in Tables 7.2 and 7.3, the numbers appearing in brackets following the estimated coefficients denote the order of difference of all the variables and the number of periods the variable has been lagged in the regression equation, and t-statistics in brackets appear below the estimated coefficients. The equation summary diagnostics are reported separately for each country equation and they include the R^2 statistic adjusted for degrees of freedom, the standard error of the estimate (SEE), the LM test for first order autocorrelation (LM) and the Ljung-

Table 7.1: Tests for Order of Integratedness of the Variables

Variable	DF/ADF I(d)	Variable	DF/ADF I(d)
QXA	-1.81 Not I(0)	ΔQXA	-12.381 I(1)
QMA	-2.43 Not I(0)	ΔQMA	-5.61 I(1)
YA	-5.66 I(0)	Not applicable	-
CA	-1.55 Not I(0)	ΔCA	-6.90 I(1)
WA	-2.43 * Not I(0)	ΔWA	-10.77 I(1)
SA	-1.07 Not I(0)	ΔSA	-5.41 I(1)
VA	-4.06 I(0)	Not applicable	-
QXB	-0.56 Not I(0)	ΔQXB	-13.50 I(1)
QMB	-1.40 * Not I(0)	ΔQMB	-8.80 I(1)
YB	-2.27 Not I(0)	ΔYB	-7.45 I(1)
WB	-1.93 Not I(0)	ΔWB	-7.19 I(1)
CB	-2.22 Not I(0)	ΔCB	-6.63 I(1)
SB	-0.05 Not I(0)	ΔSB	-4.83 I(1)
VB	-4.50 I(0)	Not applicable	-
QXC	-5.04 I(0)	Not applicable	-
QMC	-1.20 Not I(0)	ΔQMC	-9.5 I(1)
YC	-2.86 Not I(0)	ΔYC	-4.20 I(1)
WC	-2.04 Not I(0)	ΔWC	-5.22 I(1)
SC	-0.89 Not I(0))	ΔSC	-5.60 I(1)
VC	-1.38 Not I(0)	ΔSC	-4.65 I(1)
CC	-2.58 Not I(0)	ΔCC	-4.04 I(1)
QXF	-2.03 Not (0)	ΔQXF	-12.60 I(1)
QMF	-2.47 Not (1)	ΔQMF	-9.20 I(1)
YF	8.18 Not I(0)	ΔYF	-7.08 I(1)
WF	-2.37 Not I(0)	ΔWF	-6.50 I(1)
SF	-1.38 Not I(0)	ΔSF	-6.90 I(1)
VF	-3.65 I(0)	Not applicable	-
CF	-2.02 Not I(0)	ΔCF	-8.6 I(1)
QXG	1.53 Not I(0)	ΔQXG	-11.63 I(1)
QMG	1.20 Not I(0)	ΔQMG	-9.51 I(1)
YG	4.62 Not I(0)	ΔYG	-9.43 I(1)
WG	-3.07 * Not I(0)	ΔWG	-7.49 I(1)
SG	-3.44 * Not I(0)	ΔSG	-5.53 I(1)
VG	-4.01 I(0)	Not applicable -	-
CG	-2.13 Not I(0)	ΔCG	-5.76 I(1)
QXI	-2.09 Not I(0)	ΔQXI	-12.65 I(1)
QMI	1.90 Not I(0)	ΔQMI	-10.29 I(1)
YI	-2.08 * Not I(0)	ΔYI	-5.24 I(1)
WI	-1.84 Not (0)	ΔWI	-6.08 I(1)
SI	-2.73 Not I(0)	ΔSI	-6.71 I(1)
VI	-3.71 I(0)	Not applicable	-
CI	-2.64 Not I(0)	ΔCI	-4.53 I(1)
YJ	8.61 Not I(0)	ΔYI	-10.56 * I(1)
WJ	-1.8 Not I(0)	ΔWI	-6.08 I(1)
CJ	-2.95 Not(0)	ΔCI	-5.94 I(1)
QXS	-2.19 * Not I(0)	ΔQXS	-12.82 I(1)
QMS	0.70 Not I(0)	ΔQMS	-4.83 I(1)
YS	3.36 Not I(0)	ΔYS	-5.35 I(1)
WS	-4.21 I(0)	Not applicable	-
SS	-0.60 Not I(0)	ΔSS	-5.60 I(1)
VS	-4.03 I(0)	Not applicable	-
CS	-3.13 I(0)	Not applicable	-

Note: All variables are as defined in the Data Appendix. The critical values for the DF/ADF statistics are taken from Table 8.52, pp 373 in Fuller (1976). The numbers in brackets refer to the order of integration of the variables and * denotes the presence of a significant time trend.

Box (Q) test for higher order autocorrelation, the Breusch-Pagan (BP) and Engle's (ARCH) tests for heteroscedasticity and the Chow test for structural stability. Finally, the reported F statistics provide the results of testing the null hypothesis that the coefficients on the exchange rate volatility variable are equal to zero in each equation. In all cases, the number in brackets following the test statistic is its marginal significance level. The results indicate that the model performs moderately well insofar as the equations explain between one and two thirds of the variation in the dependent variables. Overall, but with some exceptions, they pass all the diagnostic tests. Specifically with regard to Table 7.2, both the LM and Q statistics indicate that autocorrelation is not a problem in any of the equations. There is, however, evidence of heteroscedasticity in the equation for Japan's trade flows to Germany, and to a lesser extent for Japan's exports to Australia. Most of the equations, with the exception of those for Germany and Italy, easily pass the Chow tests for structural constancy. With regard to Table 7.3, both the LM and Q statistics also indicate the absence of autocorrelations in any of the equations. There is, however, evidence of heteroscedasticity in the equation for Japan's imports from France, while all equations except for Japan's imports from Germany easily pass the Chow test for structural constancy.

Turning now to examine the individual coefficients, it is noteworthy that the fundamental explanatory variables are mixed in their correctness of sign and in their statistical significance. Given the focus of the paper, however, it is pertinent to examine the role of the exchange rate in detail. Generally speaking, the exchange rate variable performs well in the equations, being positively signed in nine of the 14 cases and statistically significant in seven of these. More specifically, the F statistic reported in Tables 7.2 and 7.3 reveal a statistically significant non-zero coefficient on the exchange rate volatility variable in nine of the 14 cases and statistically significant in seven of these. Of these, the majority (five) are in the import equations where they are unambiguously positively signed. Exchange rate volatility does seem to impact upon trade flows, but the overall effect is at least as likely to be positive as negative.

From a policy perspective, it would appear useful to be able to explain the different impacts of real exchange rate volatility on trade flows for the countries covered by this study. In the regression equation which captures the impact of exchange rate volatility on the volume of bilateral trade, the sign on the exchange rate volatility variable, V, depends upon several factors including the elasticity of demand and whether the firms are risk averse or risk neutral. Where the sign on the exchange rate volatility coefficient appears with a positive value,[26] this may be consistent with either a positive or a negative relationship between export supply and real exchange rate volatility (see Klein (1990)).[27] For risk averse firms, as in Hooper and Kohlhagen (1978), an increase in exchange rate volatility shifts the firm's supply curves backwards, increasing export prices and decreasing volumes. If demand is elastic, this results in a negative value for V

114

Table 7.2: Japan's Export Volume Equations

Country	$\Delta^4 S_{ik}$	$\Delta^4 W_l$	$\Delta^4 W_k$	$\Delta^4 Y_k$	$\Delta^4 C_k$	$\Delta^4 C_k$	$\Delta^4 V_{ik}$	ΔdV_{ik}	ΔdV_{ik}	ΔdQX_{ik}	ΔdQX_{ik}	ΔdQX_{ik}	ΔdQX_{ik}
Australia	0.36(1,0)	1.55(1,4)	-2.58(1,4)	-0.01(0,4)	-0.17(1,3)		3.68(0,1)	-2.74(0,4)		-.01(1,1)			
	(1.28)	(0.94)	(1.38)	(0.91)	(0.29)		(3.25)	(2.16)		(4.66)			
Britain	0.22(1,4)	5.38(1,3)	-0.22(1,0)	-0.00(1,0)	5.46(1,0)		-1.93(0,1)			-0.01(1,1)			
	(0.91)	(2.11)	(0.07)	(1.68)	(1.52)		(0.97)			(5.02)			
Canada	-0.67(1,2)	8.36(1,3)	-1.72(1,4)	-1.16(1,0)	22.67(1,3)	-22.0(1,4)	3.01(1,2)			-0.01(1,1)	-0.01(1,2)		
	(1.42)	(3.17)	(0.48)	(0.4)	(1.68)	(1.63)	(1.14)			(5.29)	(3.76)		
France	2.35(1,2)	1.41(1,4)	-4.76(1,0)	0.14(1,4)	-1.48(1,1)		2.31(0,2)	-3.57(0,3)	4.10(0,4)	0.00(1,1)			
	(1.88)	(1.35)	(2.00)	(1.58)	(2.02)		(1.68)	(2.32)	(3.04)	(3.63)			
Germany	1.91(1,4)	-4.88(1,0)	-3.76(1,3)	0.27(1,3)	3.72(1,4)		-9.70(0,0)	12.09(0,3)	9.14(0,4)	-0.00(1,1)			
	(1.67)	(1.33)	(1.75)	(0.01)	(1.66)		(2.57)	(2.88)	(2.35)	(3.95)			
Italy	2.03(1,2)	1.90(1,4)	-1.84(1,2)	0.00(1,1)	0.87(1,2)		-2.05(0,0)	-3.32(0,3)	1.72(0,4)	0.00(1,1)	0.00(1,2)	0.00(1,3)	0.00(1,4)
	(1.32)	(1.94)	(1.47)	(0.05)	(1.44)		(1.89)	(2.78)	(1.73)	(4.10)	(4.26)	(3.18)	(3.76)
US	-6.12(1,3)	40.74(1,3)	-5.13(0,2)	-0.08(1,2)	-5.69(0,2)		-21.3(0,0)			-0.00(1,1)	-0.00(1,2)	-0.00(1,3)	
	(1.64)	(1.50)	(1.12)	(0.06)	(0.054)		(0.94)			(5.14)	(2.89)	(2.78)	

Equation Diagnostics

Country	R^2	SEE	LM	Q	BP	ARCH	CHOW	F
Australia	0.37	19.70	0.49 (.48)	28.52 (.13)	37.0 (.00)	3.09 (.07)	0.62 (.76)	6.70 (.00)
Britain	0.34	30.06	0.05 (.82)	11.41 (.95)	12.4 (.13)	1.70 (.19)	0.98 (.47)	0.95 (.33)
Canada	0.42	29.59	0.97 (.32)	10.92 (.96)	9.3 (.50)	0.92 (.52)	0.01 (.91)	1.29 (.26)
France	0.35	12.28	0.18 (.66)	15.37 (.80)	7.6 (.57)	0.23 (.62)	1.18 (.33)	3.44 (.02)
Germany	0.32	39.11	0.28 (.59)	22.09 (.39)	21.5 (.00)	7.44 (.01)	4.70 (.00)	4.58 (.01)
Italy	0.69	9.98	1.03 (.31)	21.78 (.41)	21.4 (.06)	2.6 (.10)	5.80 (.00)	3.07
US	0.34	32.10	0.65 (.41)	12.93 (.91)	9.7 (.37)	0.86 (.35)	0.19 (.99)	0.35 (.36)

Table 7.3: Japan's Import Volume Equations

Country	$\Delta^d S_{ik}$	$\Delta^d W_i$	$\Delta^d W_{ik}$	$\Delta^d Y_i$	$\Delta^d C_i$	$\Delta^d Y_{ik}$	$\Delta^d V_{ik}$	$\Delta^d V_{ik}$	$\Delta^d V_{ik}$	$\Delta^d QM_{ik}$	$\Delta^d QM_{ik}$	$\Delta^d QM_{ik}$
Australia	10.15(1,1)	7.17(1,2)	-24.81(1,1)	0.00(1,3)	17.55(1,2)	16.87(0,0)	20.99(0,1)	14.30(0,2)	19.85(0,3)	-0.00(1,1)		0.00(1,4)
	(3.52)	(0.95)	(3.96)	(0.05)	(2.72)	(2.87)	(3.04)	(1.90)	(3.05)	(4.27)		(4.87)
Britain	-7.14(1,4)	-1.49(1,2)	1.32(1,1)	0.00(1,0)	-2.30(1,2)	1.01(0,4)				-.00(1,1)	0.00(1,3)	
	(1.40)	(1.67)	(2.24)	(0.70)	(2.07)	(2.28)				(3.04)	(2.45)	
Canada	2.06(1,2)	-4.85(1,4)	-0.47(1,1)	-0.00(1,2)	-5.51(1,1)	6.09(1,0)				-0.67(0,1)		
	(1.74)	(1.46)	(0.12)	(4.02)	(2.73)	(2.17)				(2.33)		
France	-4.35(1,3)	-3.26(1,0)	-8.38(1,1)	0.00(1,4)	-1.93(1,1)	3.87(0,4)				-0.00(1,1)	0.00(1,2)	
	(2.52)	(1.91)	(3.06)	(1.61)	(2.31)	(2.43)				(2.30)	(3.80)	
Germany	-1.99(1,3)	-0.78(1,1)	5.47(1,0)	-0.58(1,2)	-5.34(1,1)	-5.87(0,0)				-0.001(1,1)		
	(1.69)	(0.25)	(1.41)	(2.90)	(2.58)	(1.65)				(0.88)		
Italy	2.68(1,4)	0.65(1,3)	-0.36(1,1)	-0.00(1,1)	-0.52(1,1)	-0.69(0,0)				0.00(1,2)		
	(1.03)	(0.91)	(0.40)	(1.93)	(1.18)	(0.79)				(2.44)		
US	10.54(1,2)	-16.00(1,4)	-1.20(0,2)	-0.01(1,2)	-14.52(1,2)	17.12(0,0)	12.18(4)			-0.00(1,1)		
	(2.47)	(1.83)	(0.76)	(2.36)	(2.86)	(2.50)	(1.95)			(1.93)		

Equation Diagnostics

	R^2	SEE	LM	Q	BP	ARCH	CHOW	F
Australia	0.61	64.45	0.02 (.87)	17.20 (.70)	16.3 (.23)	0.02 (.89)	1.21 (.32)	10.18
Britain	0.39	6.63	2.31 (.13)	18.71 (.60)	14.6 (.10)	0.19 (.66)	1.87 (.09)	5.21 (.03)
Canada	0.34	39.51	0.97 (.37)	25.10 (.24)	9.3 (.50)	0.11 (.91)	.92 (.52)	4.73 (.03)
France	0.41	17.24	2.08 (.15)	10.12 (.98)	15.9 (.04)	8.20 (.00)	0.60 (.79)	5.90 (.02)
Germany	0.32	40.27	0.07 (.77)	21.30 (.44)	13.4 (.06)	1.50 (.21)	2.35 (.04)	2.71 (.11)
Italy	0.26	7.45	0.30 (.58)	32.04 (.06)	15.6 (.05)	0.05 (.87)	1.34 (.25)	0.63 (.43)
US	0.29	103.07	1.12 (.29)	23.58 (.31)	15.6 (.04)	1.39 (.24)	0.83 (.58)	4.99 (.01)

Note to the Table: The explanatory variables take the form $\Delta^d x$, where superscript d denotes the order of integration of the variable x and Δ^d denotes that x has been differenced d times to induce stationarity. The numbers in brackets after the coefficient, denotes order of difference of the variable and lag of the variable respectively. The equation summary diagnostics are (adjusted) R^2 the coefficient of determination, SEE the standard error of the estimate, LM test for first der autocorrelation, Q is the Ljung-Box test for higher order autocorrelation, the Breusch-Pagan (BP) and Engle's (ARCH) tests for heteroscedasticity and the Chow test for structural stability.

116

(since the percentage decrease in volume is greater than the percentage rise in price), while inelastic demand results in a positive value on the coefficient for V. By contrast, Giovannini (1988) demonstrates that exporting firms invoicing in their own currency may cut prices as exchange rate volatility increases. In this case the value for V is positive if demand is elastic (i.e. real exchange rate volatility stimulates export supply) and negative if demand is inelastic. To be able to distinguish between these two competing hypotheses, we require estimates of the demand elasticities for each country's export flows, but these are not available from the results presented here since the coefficient on the real exchange rate represents a combination of demand and supply elasticities. The results should not, therefore, be interpreted as unambiguous evidence that real exchange rate volatility stimulates export supply. Aschheim et al (1993)[28] demonstrates that most studies including the IMF (1984), Gotur (1985), Aschheim et al (1985, 1987), Bailey et al (1986, 1987), Koray and Lastrapes (1989) and Medhora (1990), which have rejected the hypothesis that volatility has had an adverse impact on trade, find it only for *real* exchange-rate volatility,but even here the evidence is mixed. Finally, the effect of exchange rate volatility on international trade specialisation can only be determined to the extent that it imposes a deadweight loss from under-or-over-specialisation of comparative advantage. Policy makers need to be aware of the nature of this deadweight loss when considering macroeconomic policies that affect exchange rate volatility. Perhaps of more significance here is the importance of weighing the effects of exchange-rate volatility on trade against the costs of alternatives to volatility. If volatility in exchange rates reflects shifts in underlying fundamentals, the cost of maintaining stability may be intervention in the market by the monetary authority. Over the long run, however, market intervention by the monetary authorities would be unsustainable. Trade or capital controls, or the adoption of monetary and fiscal policies could be more costly to both the domestic economy and to international trade than the costs of exchange rate volatility.

Summary and Conclusions

The purpose of this chapter has been to examine the extent to which exchange rate volatility impedes bilateral trade flows. Using an eight country dataset which spans the period 1978(1) - 1992(2), this chapter presented estimated models of bilateral trade flows in which the null hypothesis of zero exchange rate volatility effect was tested against the alternative hypothesis of non-zero volatility effect. In addition to the exchange rate volatility, other factors that were posited to affect trade flows include data on real economic activity, costs, and prices which feature in the theoretical framework . The empirical analysis differs from the majority of previous research by appropriately specifying the models in terms of the order of integration of the data and in terms of the equation dynamics. The major finding is that exchange rate volatility is at least as likely to raise trade flows as it is to impede them. Of the 14 bilateral trade flow cases, real exchange rate volatility is significantly and positively related to trade flows in six cases, five of which involve exports to Japan.

Why, in the majority of these cases, does this result pertain to exports to Japan? To answer this question, we need to focus on several factors, including the elasticity of demand, whether firms are risk averse or risk neutral, as well as the currency of denomination in which the exports are invoiced. As with previous empirical research on the relationship between exchange rate volatility and trade flows, it is difficult to draw unambiguous policy conclusions. Perhaps the most significant aspect of this work is the importance of comparing the effects of exchange-rate costs of alternative policy options which might be enacted in order to reduce it.

8 Summary, Conclusions, Policy Implications and Further Studies

Introduction

This final chapter summarises the major findings and policy implications derivable from this book. Finally suggestions for further study arising from the empirical work in the book are given. The chapter is organised as follows. We begin by providing a general review of the study. Next we point to the policy implications which emerge from the analysis. Finally, we suggests areas for further work.

General Review of the Study

The fundamental question examined by this book concerns the relationship between the volatility of financial asset prices and real economic activity. Interest in this relationship has been stimulated by a number of observations made in the financial economics literature, especially since the onset of financial deregulation in the early 1980's. In concluding, it is necessary first to reiterate the fundamental questions posed at the beginning of the book: what are the causes of financial asset volatility? What effect do Government policies via fiscal and monetary instruments have on financial asset values? Has increased exchange rate volatility in the post-float era impeded trade flows? To answer these questions, we attempt to develop empirical models to investigate the effects of financial volatility on real economic activity.

The novel analysis is primarily conducted in Chapters four to seven of the book. Chapter four considers the causes of financial market volatility in Australia by estimating an empirical model of the determinants of movements in the volatility of the Australian stock market. Chapters five and six then expand on the results from Chapter four by developing empirical models which broaden the issue of the relationship between the volatility of financial asset prices and real economic activity. Thus the analysis in Chapter five considers the effect of monetary volatility on the volatility of financial asset prices and real economic activity, while Chapter six examines the effect of innovations in fiscal financing on exchange rate volatility. Finally, Chapter seven examines the effect of exchange rate volatility on international trade flows since the introduction of flexible exchange rates in the post financial deregulation environment.

What Factors Influence Financial Volatility and Real Economic Activity?

Amongst the most important determinants of Australian stock market volatility are found to be the volatility of inflation and interest rates which are directly associated with stock market volatility, while the volatility of industrial production, the current account deficit and money supply are indirectly associated with stock market volatility. Amongst these variables, the most significant determinant of conditional volatility in the Australian stock market is the degree of volatility which exists in the money supply. By contrast, no evidence is found of a statistically significant relationship between foreign exchange market volatility and that of stock market volatility. This evidence from Chapter four suggesting that a significant linkage exists between the conditional volatility of the stock market and the conditional volatility of the money supply provided the motivation for Chapter five.

Chapter five examined the extent to which monetary growth volatility is transmitted to the real sector of the macroeconomy. Using a monthly Australian dataset (including the money supply, the foreign exchange and interest rate, inflation and real output) a Markowitz efficient portfolio was constructed comprising bonds, stocks and foreign exchange to eliminate diversifiable financial risk associated with holding these assets. The portfolio therefore contains only nondiversifiable risk and it is intuitive that this should be the transmission mechanism that is examined in a modern financial system. The major findings suggest the following: *firstly*, the models find strong evidence of a statistically significant direct transmission mechanism from higher (lower) monetary volatility to higher (lower) real output volatility. *Secondly*, when financial assets are included separately in the model rather than in the efficient portfolio, higher (lower) monetary volatility is associated with lower (higher) share market and interest rate volatility and with higher (lower) foreign exchange market volatility. *Finally*, the models indicate that the transmission of monetary volatility impulses to real output occurs predominantly through the share market rather than through interest rates, with no significant effect operating through the foreign exchange market.

Evidence from Chapter four suggests no statistically significant relationship exists between foreign exchange market volatility and stock market volatility. Further evidence from Chapter five tends to vindicate the view that the volatility associated with floating exchange rates does not seem to spill over to real output. Both findings provided the motivation for investigating whether fiscal policy contributes to financial asset volatility. Here, it is interesting to note the nonexistence of recent empirical work investigating possible linkages between fiscal financing and the consequences for exchange rate movements. From a theoretical perspective, the difficulty faced by the authorities engaged with the operation of fiscal policy is the uncertainty of both the magnitude and direction of the response of financial asset prices (i.e. exchange rates) to fiscal financing initiatives. This uncertainty is more apparent under a flexible exchange rate system, where a considerable range of variation can exist depending on the precise model specification as was alluded to in the book. Chapter six concludes that the overall volatility of the exchange rate in response to innovations in fiscal financing decisions is significant in magnitude and duration for the countries considered. The point here is that while the perceived benefits of flexible exchange rates include the insulation of the domestic economy from foreign shocks and the potential for independent policy action, the more volatile exchange rate environment since the introduction of floating exchange rates appears to be significantly associated with the conduct of government policy.

Finally, in order to directly test the effects of financial asset price volatility on real economic activity, Chapter seven employed an empirical analysis to examine the extent to which exchange rate volatility impedes bilateral trade flows. Using the most current available data, a consistent set of industry-specific bilateral trade volume and price data for eight countries was used to estimate the effects of exchange rate volatility on Japan's bilateral. The empirical analysis differs from previous related empirical research by appropriately specifying the model in terms of order of integration of the data and in terms of the equation dynamics. The major finding of this analysis is that the effect of exchange rate volatility on Japan's bilateral trade flows is as least as likely to raise trade flows as it is to impede them.

Policy Implications

The evidence for stock market efficiency is not convincing; the evidence that stock prices do not always reflect fundamental values is confirmed by recent econometric testing, while periodic extreme movements in volatility are difficult to associate with changes in fundamental values. Since financial markets serve an important role in the allocation of capital, the goal of any new regulations should be to promote reforms or changes which serve to move stock prices closer to fundamental values. In practice, what would this entail? It should be understood that apart from foreign exchange or monetary policy operations, financial policy rarely takes the form of direct government purchases/sales intervention in a market. Financial policy affects the market via rules for exchange trading and dealer/market-maker behaviour, rules of disclosure and sales practice, to mention but a few. Since the October 1987 stock market crash, new rules have been introduced covering trading halts which come into effect when the market falls below a limited amount; these are known as circuit breakers. On balance there is no strong empirical or theoretical research that such rules can in fact reduce stock price volatility.

This book demonstrated that government actions via monetary and fiscal policies have potentially important direct and indirect effects on financial and real economic volatility. Higher financial volatility as demonstrated in the book may effect economic decisions to the determinant of allocational efficiency. Amongst the most important determinants of Australian stock market volatility were found to be the volatility of inflation and interest rates which are directly associated with stock market volatility, while the volatility of industrial production, the current account deficit and money supply are indirectly associated with stock market volatility. Monetary policy has a prime objective in controlling inflation which may, however, be compromised by other objectives such as keeping unemployment low. Interest rates is one area where governments appear to have more direct control. It is here, however, that the policy objective of reducing stock market volatility (via reduction in interest rate volatility) may have to take second place to other macroeconomic goals, as Australia has all too frequently experienced over the past decade.

Amongst the major findings having implications for the conduct of monetary policy are *firstly*, that higher monetary volatility is associated with lower volatility of financial asset prices and higher real output volatility and *secondly*, that monetary volatility is transmitted to real output volatility predominantly through the share market with no foreign exchange effect. The question of whether the Government controls the money supply is today highly questionable, given most industrialised countries' experience with monetary targeting. The more important question for policy makers is how to reduce monetary volatility when control over money supply appears outside its grasp. This question is important in the current context since the empirical evidence indicates that higher monetary volatility is associated with higher real output volatility. Today, policy makers would appear to be looking for answers by no longer attempting to control the money supply directly but indirectly *via* interest rate policy. *Finally*, the result that the transmission of monetary volatility impulses to real output occurs predominantly through the share market has policy implications. The result verifies international evidence that suggest changes in money supply has direct and indirect significant impacts on changes in share prices and that volatility in share prices impacts on fluctuations in real output. This evidence suggests that monetary authorities can affect the volatility of share prices and that policy makers need to consider this.

The result that fiscal policy actions have significant effects on financial asset volatility (i.e. exchange rates) is of significance to policy makers. To the extent that policy influences volatility, by having either the desired dampening effect or the undesired volatility-magnifying effect, there appears from the analysis conducted here that there is a connection running from policy to volatility. What appears interesting from the results is that no uniform response appears to be evident across the major industrialised countries over which the effects of fiscal financing innovations on exchange rates were examined. The reason for this is perhaps related to the variety of political economic structures operating in these countries.

Further Studies

Results from this book suggest that the most important determinants of Australian stock market volatility are found to be the volatility of inflation and interest rates which are directly associated with stock market volatility, while the volatility of industrial production, the current account deficit and money supply are indirectly associated. Amongst these variables, the most significant determinant of conditional volatility in the Australian stock market is the degree of volatility which exists in the money supply. A formal test of these relationships has not been attempted in this book, however further investigation along this line would appear to provide us with a clearer picture as to whether inflation and interest rate volatility are responsible for the documented evidence (see Kearns and Pagan 1993) which shows that Australian stock market volatility appears to have significantly increased over the last two decades.

A interesting finding relates to the lack of any significant relationship between foreign exchange market volatility and that of stock market volatility. This is all the more interesting in that deregulation of the financial system, and the associated floating of the exchange rate, would imply that the Australian stock market is more sensitive to international financial markets. The effect on volatility of increasing links between national stock markets is not tested in the book. Further work in the direction of examining the international transmission of Australian stock market volatility with a view to determining the links between national stock markets would appear to provide answers to the effects on the increased internationalisation of the Australian stock market.

Finally, this book found that fiscal policy actions have significant effects on financial asset volatility (i.e. exchange rates). An area of further work concerns the extent to which policy may reduce the volatility of financial asset returns in particular with respect to exchange rates and short-term interest rates.

Endnotes

Chapter 2

[1] The rate of return is the change in price plus the dividend received by stockholders during the period, all divided by the price of the investment at the beginning of the period.

[2] Contrarian traders go against the market by buying in bear markets and selling in bull markets. The relevant issue is whether contrarian activities lead to an increase in volatility. One way to examine the issue is to ask the question what would happen to stock prices if they did not enter the market. It is conceivable that market rises and declines would be larger then they are, as contrarian traders actions prevent prices from spiraling in one direction. Schwert(1990a) shows that the number of extreme price reversals has not been very high over recent years.

[3] Evidence from the U.S. on the relationship between 'options' introduction and volatility indicate a significant fall in stock return volatility after the introduction of 'options'. See Conrad (1989), Damodaran and Lim (1991) and Skinner (1989). Precise reasons for the decline are unknown, but the arrival of private information, an increase in information processing and reduced transaction costs are likely candidates. Available evidence on the effects of Index Futures introduction on market volatility, suggests that stock market volatility does not increase. See Gerety and Mulherin (1991) and Hodgson and Nicholls (1991).

[4] See Hamilton (1994), p.664.

[5] The skewness of a variable Yt with mean μ is represented by $\dfrac{E(Yt-\mu)^3}{[Var(Yt)]^{3/2}}$. A variable with a negative skew is more likely to be far below the mean than it is to be far above the mean. The kurtosis is $\dfrac{E(Yt-\mu)^4}{[Var(Yt)]^2}$. A distribution whose kurtosis exceeds 3 has more mass in the tails than a Gaussian distribution with the same variance.

[6] Daly (1997) also used the Schwert measure to examine the conditional volatility of the Australian Stock Market, Chapter four of this thesis, which is also published in the Proceedings of the International Conference on Finance, Alaska, 1997.

Chapter 3

[7] The stock market is considered to be efficient if, on average, stock prices are equal to their fundamental economic values, and past information cannot be used to develop trading rules which identify and exploit deviations from fundamental prices and thereby allow a rational investor to reliably earn excess profits.

[8] Kupiec (1993) provides a thorough review of the huge literature on stock market efficiency.

[9] Excess returns are defined as the monthly stock return less the market return.

[10] Tests carried out by Shiller (1981b) and LeRoy and Porter (1981) examined the variance restrictions imposed in the present value models of stock prices. All found rejections of the variance restrictions, Shiller concluding that the stock market was too volatile. LeRoy and Porter also suggested that the market could be too volatile and/or the present value model with constant discount rates had been rejected.

[11] Fama (1976) provides a review of these studies or at least those which generally support his definition of an efficient market. Alternately, LeRoy's (1989) review provides exceptions to studies cited by Fama.

[12] Minsky uses the term 'hedge finance' to mean borrowing for purposes with a high probability of generating adequate cash flow to service the debt in all future periods; "speculative finance" means borrowing for purposes with a high probability of providing adequate cash flow to service the debt after some time though not initially, albeit with positive expected net present value, and "Ponzi finance" means borrowing for purposes having negative expected net present value.

[13] Sundararajan and Balino (1991) give a list of cases of bank collapses and lending cutbacks that marked the end of most developing countries financial liberalization experiments.

[14] Their explanation for this phenomenon relates to the length of time which both countries had taken to readjust to the major wartime disturbance of the monetary relations. In both countries, the disturbance appeared in the form of a sharp decline in the velocity of circulation of money, that is a larger rise in money than in income.

[15] Friedman and Schwartz view is that average growth of output over long periods is determined by real factors such as natural resource endowment, social institutions, human capacities, technology, invention, enterprise and thrift. Over shorter periods, output growth will also be affected by real factors, but only to the extent that over such periods output will be affected by unanticipated changes in nominal magnitudes.

[16] What of course the monetary authorities should do according to monetarists is adopt a rule that would allow the money supply to grow at a rate of x percent a year, adhere to this rule and ignore the state of the economy.

[17] John Maynard Keynes, 'On The Theory of a Monetary Economy', in Festschrift fur Arthur Spiethoff (Munich: Duncher & Humblot, 1933); reprinted in Nebraska Journal of Economics and Business Vol. 2, No.2 Autumn 1963.

[18] In modelling a Post Keynesian macro model of the UK economy, Arestis (1995. pp.550) points out that: 'The argument widely accepted in Post Keynesian circles

is that the demand for (new) bank lending is determined by the financing requirements of the private sector and thus by other variables in the economic system such as the growth of nominal GDP'. The above arguments clearly imply that from a Post Keynesian perspective money is an endogenous variable, central banks cannot directly control the stock of money, which is determined by previously made decisions on credit and loans. It makes no sense to control an aggregate that is a consequence rather than a cause of economic activity.

[19] One exception is work by Tarhan (1993), who examined the connection between volatility and policy in the context of open market operations in the US market and sterilized intervention in the foreign exchange market.

Chapter 6

[20] The tests are conducted over the period from 1975(2) to 1995(2). The critical values are -2.57 for both Dickey-Fuller and Phillips-Perron tests. The critical values for the Dickey Fuller statistics are taken from Table 8.5.2, pp. 373 in Fuller (1976) and Table VI of Dickey-Fuller (1981, p. 1063), for the Phillips-Perron critical values see Phillips (1987) and Phillips and Perron (1988).

Chapter 7

[21] Giovannini (1988) compares this result with the analysis of the 'portfolio problem' in Rothschild and Stiglitz (1971). There, expected utility is affected by the amount invested in a risky asset, the demand for which does not necessarily decrease as its riskiness increases.

[22] In the model, firms are assumed to plan their activities over a horizon which exceeds the usual contract period. The firm is interested not only in the profitability of the present but also future contracts. The latter cannot be fully hedged either because contract values and prices are unknown and/or because the necessary set of forward exchange markets does not exist.

[23] Since there is no reliable way to predict the timing and magnitude of future changes in exchange rates, our results would most probably understate the effects of exchange rate uncertainty on trade. Furthermore, Akhtar and Hilton (1984), argue that any variability measure is likely to understate "true" uncertainty. Their discussion of uncertainty effects cannot be fully separated from those of exchange rate changes *per se*. For more details on uncertainty and exchange rate volatility see Akhtar and Hilton (1984).

[24] This involves taking into account lags as long as four quarters (Cushman, 1983; IMF, 1984) to eight quarters (Bailey et al, 1986; H-K, 1984; Gotur, 1985; Kenen and Rodrick, 1986).

[25] In a majority of empirical studies in this area, an income/output variable for the importing country only is included amongst the explanatory variables. See Bini-

Smaghi (1991), Bailey et al (1986), Chowdhury (1993), Cushman (1983,1986), Bini-Smaghi (1991), Aschheim *et al* (1985, 1987), Bailey *et al* (1986, 1987), Hooper and Kohlagen (1978), Klein (1990), Kenen and Rodrik (1990), Kroner and Lastrapes (1993), Bini-Smaghi (1991).

[26] Several recent theoretical studies (Viaene and de Vries (1992), Dellas and Zilberfarb (1993) and Giovannini (1988) have examined this aspect of trade flows and exchange rate volatility.

[27] Klein's study found that in six of the nine categories of goods exported from the US to seven industrial countries, the volatility of the real exchange rate significantly affects the value of exports and in five of these categories the effect is positive.

[28] Aschheim et al (1987), tested the impact of exchange-rate volatility on real exports of eleven OECD countries using two measures of volatility for both real and nominal exchange rates. Considering only real exchange rate volatility over the managed floating period, they found three out of sixteen cases in which exchange-rate volatility negatively and significantly affected real exports.

Bibliography

Arestis, P. (1988), "Post-Keynesian Theory of Money, Credit and Finance," in P. Arestis (ed.), *Post-Keynesian Monetary Economics,* Edward Elgar Publishing, 41-71.

Arestis, P. and A.S. Eichner (1988), "The Post-Keynesian and Institutionalist Theory of Money and Credit," Journal of Economic Issues, Vol XXII, No 4, December.

Akaike, H. (1974), "A New Look at the Statistics Model Identification," IEEE transactions on Automatic Control AC-19, 716-723.

Akhtar, M.A. and Spence Hilton, R., (1984), "Exchange Rate Uncertainty and International Trade: Some Conceptual Issues and New Estimates for Germany and the United States," Federal Reserve Bank of New York Research, Paper No. 8403.

Al-Saji, A.K. (1992), "Unemployment, Money Growth and interest Rate Volatility in Italy and the United Kingdom," Rivista Internazionale di Scienze Economiche e Commerciali, XXXIX, July, 607-615.

Al-Saji, A.K. (1994), "The Effects of Money Growth and Interest Rate Volatility on Output: Empirical Evidence from a Developing Country," Studi Economici, 51, 3.

Aliben, R.Z. (1976), "The Firm Under Pegged and Floating Exchange Rates," Scandinavian Journal of Economics, 78, 309-332.

Allen, F. and G.Gorton. (1993), "Churning Bubbles," Review of Economic Studies, October; 60(4), 813-836.

Allen, Franklin and Douglas Gale (1994), "Limited Market Participation and Volatility of Asset Prices," American Review Economic, September, 84, 4, 933-955.

Allen, Franklin and Gary Gorton (1993), "Churning Bubbles," Review of Economic Studies, October, 60, 4, 813-837.

Andersen, T.G. (1992), "A Model of Return Volatility and Trading Volume," Working Paper, Northwestern University, Evanston, IL.

Aschheim, J., Bailey, M.J., and Tavlas, G.S. (1985), "Dollar Appreciation, Deficit Stimulation, and New Protectionism," Journal of Policy Modeling, 7, 107-21.

Aschheim, J., Bailey, M.J., and Tavlas, G.S. (1987), "Dollar Variability, the New Protectionism, Trade and Financial Performance," in D. Salvatore (ed.), The New Projectionist Threat to World Welfare, New York: Holland, 425-44.

Aschheim, J., Tavlas, G.S. and Ulan. M., (1993),"The relationship between exchange rate variability and protection," in D.Salvatore (ed.), Protection and world welfare, Cambridge University Press, 290-308.

Asseery, A.and D.A. Peel, (1991), "The Effects of Exchange Rate Volatility on Exports," Economic Letters, 37, 173-177.

Attansio, O.P. and Wadhwani, S., (1989), "Risk and predictability of stock market returns," Unpublished manuscript. (Department of Economics, Stanford University, Palo Alto, CA.)

Bailey, M.J., Tavlas, G.S. and Ulan, M., (1986), "Exchange Rate Variability and Trade Performance Evidence for the Big Seven Industrial Countries," Weltwirtschaftliches Archiv, 122, 466-77.

Bailey, M.J., Tavlas, G.S. and Ulan, M., (1987), "The Impact of Exchange Rate Volatility on Export Growth: Some Theoretical Considerations and Empirical Results," Journal of Policy Modelling, 9, 225-43.

Baillie, R.T. and Bollerslev, T., (1990), "A multivariate generalised ARCH approach to modeling risk premiain foreign exchange rate markets," Journal of International Money and Finance, 9, 309-324.

Baillie, R.T. and DeGennaro, R.P., (1990), "Stock returns and volatility." Journal of Financial and Quantitative Analysis, 25, 203-214.

Balassa, B., (1979), "Trade Uncertainty Under Flexible Exchange Rates," in Swoboda, A.K., (ed.), Managing International Financial Relations in a World of Uncertainty. Proceedings of the Fourth Conference of the International Center for Monetary and Banking Studies, December, 1976 (Geneva: Institut Universitaire de Hautes Etudes Internationales).

Balke, Nathan, S. and Robert J. Gordon, (1989), "The Estimation of Pre-War GNP: Methodology and New Evidence," Journal of Political Economy, 97, February, 38-92.

Baron, D.P., (1976), "Fluctuating Exchange Rates and the Pricing of Exports," Economic Inquiry, 1A, 425-438.

Barro, R.J. (1974), "Are Government Bonds Net Wealth?," Journal of Political Economy, 82, 1095-1117.

Barro, R.J. (1978), "Unanticipated Money, Output, and the Price Level in the United States," Journal of Political Economy, 86, August, 549-580.

Barro, R.J. (1981), Money, Expectations, and the Business Cycle. New York: Academic Press.

Bayoumi, T. and B. Eichengreen, (1994), "Macroeconomic Adjustment Under Bretton Woods and the Post Bretton Woods Float - An Impulse Response Analysis," Economic Journal, July, 104(425), 813-827.

Bebchuk, L.A. and J.C. Fershtman, (1994), "Insider Trading and the Managerial Choice among Risky Projects," Journal of Financial and Quantitative Analysis, March, 29(1), 1-14.

Belongia, Michael T. (1984), "Money Growth Variability and GNP," Federal Reserve Bank of St Louis Review, April, 66, 23-31.

Bera, A.K. and M.L. Higgins, (1993), "ARCH Models:Properties, Estimation and Testing," Journal of Economic Surveys 7, 305-366.

Berry, T.D. and K.M. Howe, (1994), "Public Information Arrival," Journal of Finance, September; 49(4),1331-1346.

Bini-Smaghi, L., (1991), "Exchange Rate Variability and Trade: Why is it so difficult to find any empirical relationship?," Applied Economics, 23, 927-936.

Black, F., and Scholes, M. (1973), "The Pricing of Options and Corporate Liabilities, Journal of Political Economy, 3, 133-155.

Black, F. (1976), "Studies of Stock Price Volatility Changes," in Proceedings of the 1976. Meetings of the Business and Economics Statistics Section, American Statistical Association, 177-181.

Black, S.W., (1977), Floating Exchange Rates and the Conduct of Macroeconomic Policy, Yale University Press, New Haven.

Bollerslev, T. (1986), "Generalised Autoregressive Conditional Heteroskedasticity," Journal of Econometrics, 31, 307-327.

Bollerslev, T, Chou, R.Y. and Kroner, K.F., (1992), "ARCH Modelling in Finance: A Review of the Theory and Empirical Evidence," Journal of Econometrics, April/May, 52, 5-29.

Boyer, R.S. and Hodrick, R.J. (1982), "Perfect Foresight, Financial Policy and Exchange Rate Dynamics," Canadian Journal of Economy, 15, 143-164.

Brailsford, T.J. and Faff, R.W. (1993), "Modelling Australian Stock Market Volatility," Australian Journal of Management, 18, 2, 109-132.

Branson, W.H. (1977), "Asset Markets and Relative Prices in Exchange Rate Determination," Sozialwissenschaftliche Annalen, 1, 69-89.

Branson, W.H. and Buiter, W. (1983), "Monetary and Fiscal Policy with Flexible Exchange Rates," in J.S. Bhandari and B.H. Putnam (eds.), Economic Interdependence and Flexible Exchange Rates, Cambridge, MIT Press, MA. 251-285.

Calamanti, A. (1983), "The Securities Market and Underdevelopment," North Holland, Amsterdam.

Camerer, C. (1989), "Bubbles and Fads in Asset Prices," Journal of Economic Surveys, Vol.3, No 1.

Campa, J.M. (1993), "Entry By Foreign Firms in the United States Under Exchange Rate Uncertainty," Review of Economics and Statistics, November, 75(4), 614-622.

Campbell, J.Y. (1987), "Stock returns and term structure," Journal of Financial Economics, 18, 373-399.

Campbell, J.Y., Lo, A.W. and MacKinlay, A.C. (1997), "The Econometrics of Financial Markets," Princeton University Press.

Campbell, J.Y. and Hentschel, L. (1993), "No news is good news: An asymmetric model of changing volatility in stock returns," Journal of Financial Economics, 31, 281-318.

Campbell, J.Y. and Kyle, A.S. (1993), "Smart Money, Noise Trading and Stock Price Behaviour," Review of Economic Studies, January, 60, 1, 1-34.

Campbell, J.Y. and Shiller, R. J. (1988), "Stock Prices, Earnings and Expected Dividends," Journal of Finance, July; 43(3), 661-676.

Caporale. T. and Doroodian, K. (1994), "Exchange Rate Variability and the Flow of International Trade," Economic Letters, September; 46(1), 49-54.

Chada, Binky (1989), "Is Increasing Price Flexibility Stabilising?," Journal of Money, Credit and Banking, November; 21, 481-497.

Chan, K.C., Karolyi, G.A. and Stulz, R.M. (1992), "Global Financial Markets and the Risk Premium on US Equity," Journal of Financial Economics, 32, 137-167.

Chang, E.C. and Pinegar, J. M. (1989), "Seasonal Fluctuations in Industrial Production and Stock Market Seasonals," Journal of Financial and Quantitative Analysis, 24, 59-74.

Chang, E.C. and Pinegar, J. M. (1990), "Stock Market Seasonal and Prespecified Multifactor Pricing Relations," Journal of Financial and Quantitative Analysis," 25, 517-533.

Chen, N., Roll, R. and Ross, S. A. (1986),"Economic Forces and the Stock Market," Journal of Business, Vol.59, 383-403.

Chou, R.Y. (1988), "Volatility persistence and stock valuations: Some critical empirical evidence using GARCH," Journal of Applied Econometrics, 3, 279-294.

Chowdhury, A.R. (1993), "Does Exchange Rate Volatility Depress Trade Flows? Evidence from Error Correction Models," Review of Economics and Statistics, November; 75(4), 700-706.

Christie, A.A. (1982), "The Stochastic Behaviour of Common Stock Variances: Value, Leverage and Interest Rate Effects," Journal of Financial Economics, 10, 407-432.

Clark, P.B. (1973) "Uncertainty, Exchange Risk, and the Level of International Trade," Western Economic Journal, 3, 27-48.

Clark, P. (1979) "Investment in the 1970s: Theory, Performance and Predictions," Brookings Papers on Economic Activity, 1, 73-113.

Collinge, R.A. (1994) "Dampening Exchange Rate Volatility - a Micro Alternative to Macro Policies," Journal of Policy Modeling, February; 16(1), 113-118.

Connolly, R.A. and Taylor, W.A., (1990), "The impact of central bank intervention on spot foreign exchange market volatility," Unpublished manuscript. (Graduate school of Business, University of North Carolina, Chapel Hill, N.C.)

Cuddington, J.J, P., Johansson and Ohlsson, J. (1985), "Optimal Policy Rules and Regime Switching in Disequilibrium Models," Journal of Public Economics, 27(2), 247-254.

Cuddington, J.J. and Vinals, J.M. (1986a), "Budget Deficits and the Current Account in the Presence of Classical Unemployment," Economic Journal, 96, 101-119.

Cuddington, J.J. and Vinals, J.M. (1986b), "Budget Deficits and the Current Account: An Intertemporal Disequilibrium Approach," Journal of International Economics, 21, 1-24.

Cunningham, S.R. and Vilasuso, J. (1994) "Comparing the United States GNP Volatility Across Exchange Rate Regimes - An Application of Saphe Cracking," Journal of Macroeconomics, Summer; 16(3), 445-459.

Cushman, D.O. (1983), "The Effects of Real Exchange Rate Risk on International Trade," Journal of International Economics, 15, 45-63.

Cushman, D.O. (1986), "Has Exchange Risk Depressed International Trade? The Impact of Third-Country Exchange Risk," Journal of International Money and Finance, 5, 361-379.

Daly, K.J. (1996a), "Fiscal Financing and Exchange Rate Volatility: An Australian Empirical Analysis," Economic Papers, Vol 15, No.1, March, 10-20.

Daly, K.J. (1996b), "Australian Financial Volatility: An Empirical Investigation," Third International Conference on Economics in Business and Government. Published by The Economics Society of Australia (Queensland).

Daly, K.J. (1997), "The Causes of Stock Market Volatility in Australia," Third International Conference on Financial Econometrics. Juneau, Alaska, July.

Daly, K.J. (1997a), "The Effect of Exchange Rate Volatility on the Volume of Japan's Bilateral Trade," Singapore Economic Review, Vol. 41 No.2 October.

Daly, K.J., (1998), "Exchange Rate Volatility and International Trade Flows: Empirical Evidence for Australia," in S. Paul (ed.), Trade and Growth, Allen and Unwin, 105-134.

Darrat, A.F. (1988), "On Fiscal Policy and the Stock Market," Journal of Money, Credit and Banking, 20, 353-363.

Darrat, A.F. (1990), "Stock Returns, Money and Fiscal Deficits," Journal of Quantitative Analysis, 25, 387-398.

Davidian, M. and Carroll, R.J. (1987), "Variance Function Estimation," Journal of the American Statistical Association, 82, 1079-1091.

Davidson, J.E.H., Hendry, D.F., Srba, F. and Yeo, S. (1978), "Econometric Modelling of the Aggregate Time Series Relationship Between Consumers' Expenditure and Income in the United Kingdom," Economic Journal, 88, 661-692.

De Grauwe, P. and Bernard de Bellefroid,(1987), "Long-Run Exchange Rate Variability and International Trade," in Sven W. Arndt and J. David Richardson ed. Real-Financial Linkages among Open Economies, MIT Press, 193-212.

De Long, J., Bradford, G. and Summers , L.H. (1986), "Is Increased Price Flexibility Stabilizing?," American Economic Review, December, 76, 1031-1044.

De Long, J., Dhleifer, A., Summers, L.H. and Waldman, R.J. (1989), "The size and incidence of the losses from noise trading," Journal of Finance, XLIV(3), 681-96.

De Long, J. Bradford et al (1990), "Noise Trader Risk in Financial Markets," Journal of Political Economy, June; 91(3), 401-419.

de Jong, F. Kemna, A. and Kloek, T. (1990), "The impact of option expirations on the Dutch stock market," Unpublished manuscript (Erasmus University, Rotterdam).

Denhertog, R.G.J. (1994), "Pricing of Permanent and Transitory Volatility for United States," Economic Letters, April; 44(4), 421-426.

Dhakal, G. Kandil, F. and Sharma, T. (1993), "Stock Market Volatility and Fundamentals," Journal of Financial Economics, 35, 67-89.

Dickey, D.A. & Fuller, W.A., (1981) "Likelihood Ratio Statistics for Autoregressive Time Series with a Unit Root," Econometrica, 53, 251-276.

Dickey, D.A., (1976), "Estimation and Hypothesis Testing for Nonstationary Time Series," PhD Dissertation. Iowa State University.

Dickey, D. and Fuller, W.A. (1979), "Distribution of the Estimators for Time Series Regressions with a Unit Root," Journal of the American Statistical Association, 74, 427-431.

Dickey, D.A. & Fuller, W.A., (1981), "Likelihood Ratio Statistics for Autoregressive Time Series with a Unit Root," Econometrica, 53, 251-276.

Diebold, F.X. and Nerlove, M. (1989), "The Dynamics of Exchange Rate Volatility: A Multivariate Latent Factor ARCH Model," Journal of Applied Econometrics, 4, 1-21.

Diebold, F.X. and Pauly, P. (1988b), "Has the EMS reduced member country exchange rate volatility?," Empirical Economics, 13, 81-102.

Diebold, F.X. and Pauly, P. (1988a), "Endogenous risk in a portfolio balance rational expectations model of the Deutschmark dollar rate," European Economic Review, 32, 27-53.

Diebold, F.X and Lopez, J.A. (1995), "Modeling Volatility Dynamics," in K.D. Hoover (ed), Macroeconometrics; Developments, Tensions and Prospects, Kluwer Academic Publishers, Boston.

Diebold Dellas, H. and B.Z. Zilberfarb, (1993), "Real Exchange Rate Volatility and International Trade: A Reexamination of the Theory," Southern Economic Journal, Vol 59, No. 4, 641-47.

Dolado, J. & Jenkinson, T. (1987) Cointegration: A survey of recent developments. Applied Economics discussion Paper, No. 39. University of Oxford.

Domowitz, I. and Hakkio, C.S., (1985), "Conditional variance and the risk premium in the foreign exchange market," Journal of International Economics, 19, 47-66.

Dornbusch, R. (1976), "Expectations and Exchange Rate Dynamics," Journal of Political Economy, 84, 101-119.

Dornbusch, R. (1988), "Real Exchange Rates and Macroeconomics: A Selective Survey," National Bureau of Economic Research Working Paper, No. 2775, November.

Dornbusch, R. and Fischer, S. (1980), "Exchange Rates and the Current Account," American Economic Review, 70, 960-971.

Driskill, Robert A. and Steven M. Sheffrin (1986), "Is Price Flexibility Destabilising?" American Economic Review, 76, September, 802-807.

Dutkowsky, D.H., (1987), "Unanticipated Money Growth, Interest Rate Volatility, and Unemployment in the United States," The Review of Economics and Statistics, LXIX, February, 144-148.

Dwyer, G.P. (1985), "Federal Deficits, Interest Rates and Monetary Policy", Journal of Money, Credit and Banking, XVII, 2, 655-681.

Dwyer, L., Duc-Tho Nguyen and Suri.Rajapakse, (1996), "The Volatility of Australia's Exchange Rate: A Synthesis," Economic Analysis and Policy, March; 26,1.

Eden, B. and B.Jovanovic, (1994), "Asymmetric Information and the Excess Volatility of Stock Prices", Economic Inquiry, April; 32(2), 228-235.

Edwards, F.R. (1988), "Policies to Curb Stock Market Volatility," Working Paper Series CSFM No. 176, Center for the Study of Futures Markets, Columbia. Business School.

Engle, R.F. (1982), "Autoregressive Conditional Heteroscedasticity with Estimates of the Variance of UK Inflation," Econometrica, 50, 987-1008.

Engle, R.F. (1983), "Estimates of the varianceof U.S. inflation based on the ARCH model," Journal of Money, Credit and Banking, 15, 286-301.

Engle, R.F. (1993), "Statistical Models for Financial Volatility," Financial Analysts Journal, 49(1), 72-78.

Engle,R.F., and Bollerslev, T. "Modelling the Persistence of Conditional Variances," Econometric Review," 5, 1-50.

Engle,R.F., and Gonzalez-Rivera. (1991), "Semiparametric Arch models," Journal of Business and Economic Statistics, 9, 391-359.

Engle, R.F., Hendry, D.F. and Trumble, D. (1985), "Small sample properties of ARCH estimators and tests," Canadian Journal of Economics, 18, 66-93.

Engle, R.F., Lilian, D. and Robins, R. (1987), "Estimating Time Varying Risk Premia in theTerm Structure; The ARCH-M Model," Econometrica, 55, 391-407.

Engle, R.F. and Mustafa, C.M. (1992), "Implied ARCH Models from Option Prices," Journal of Econometrics, 52, 289-311.

Engle, R.F. and Rodrigues, A.P. (1989), "Tests of International CAPM with time-varying covariances," Journal of Applied Econometrics, 4, 119-138.

Ethier, W., (1973), "International Trade and the Forward Exchange Market," American Economic Review, 63, 494-503.

Evans, P., (1984), "The Effects on Output of Money Growth and Interest Rate Volatility in the United States," Journal of Political Economy, April, 92, 204-222.

Fama, E.F., (1965), "The behaviour of stock market prices," Journal of Business, 38, 34-105.

Fama, E.F. (1970), "Efficient Capital Markets: A Review of Theory and Empirical Work," Journal of Finance, May, 25, 383-417.

Fama, E.F. (1976), "Foundations of Finance: Portfolio Decisions and Securities Prices," New York: Basic Books.

Fama, E.F., and Schwert, G.W. (1977), "Asset returns and inflation," Journal of Business, 38, 34-105.

Fama, E.F. (1990), "Stock Returns, Expected Returns and Real Activity," Journal of Finance, 45, 1089-1108.

Fama, Eugene F. (1970), "Efficient Capital Markets:A Review of Theory and Empirical Work," Journal of Finance, May; 25(2), 383-417.

Flavin, M. (1983), "Excess Volatility in Financial Markets: A Reassessment of Empirical Evidence," Journal of Political Economy, 91, 929-956.

Figlewski, S. (1996), "Forecasting Volatility," New York University, Stern School of Business.

Fisher, I. (1923), "The Business Cycles Largely a Dance of the Dollar," Journal of the American Statistical Association, December, 1923, 18, 1024-1028.

Frank,G. (1988), "Exchange Rate Volatility and International Trade", Journal of International Economics.

French, K.R. and Roll, R. (1986), "Stock Return Variance: The Arrival of Information and the Reaction of Traders," Journal of Financial Economics, 17, 5-26.

French, K.R., Schwert, G.W and Staumbaugh, R.F. (1987), "Expected Stock Returns and Volatility", Journal of Financial Economics, 19, 3-29.

Frenkel, J.A. and Meese, R. (1987), "Are Exchange Rates Excessively Variable?" in Stanley Fischer, ed. NBER macroeconomics annual: 1987, Cambridge, MIT Press, 117-53.

Frenkel, J.A. and Razin, A. (1986), "Fiscal Policies in the World Economy", Journal of Political Economy, 94, 564-594.

Friedman, M. and A.J. Schwartz (1963), "A monetary history of the United States, 1867-1960," Princeton: Princeton University Press for NBER.

Friedman, M. and A.J. Schwartz (1982), "Monetary Trends in the United States and the United Kingdom,"University of Chicargo Press for NBER.

Friedman. B.M. and Laibson, D.I. (1989), "Economic Implications of Extraordinary Movements in Stock Prices," Brookings Papers on Economic Activity, 2, 137-189.

Fuller, W.A. (1976), Introduction to Statistical Time Series, New York, Wiley.

Galeotti, M. and Schiantarelli, F. (1994). "Stock Market Volatility and Investment - Do only Fundamentals Matter," Economica, May; 61(242), 147-165.

Gallant, A.R. Hsieh, D.A. and Tauchen, G. (1989), "On fitting a recalcitrant series: the pound/dollar exchange rate, 1974-1983, in Barnett, W.A., Powell, J. and Tauchen, G. (eds.), Nonparametric and Semiparametric Methods in Econometrics and Statistics, Cambridge University Press, Cambridge.

Gallant, A.R., Rossi, P.E. and Tauchen, G. (1990), "Stock prices and volume, Unpublished manuscript (Department of Economics, Duke University, Durham, N.C.)

Gennotte, G. and Leland, H. (1990), "Market Liquidity, Hedging and Crashes," American Economic Review, December; 80(5), 999-1021.

Gertler, M. (1988), "Financial Structure and Aggregate Economic Activity," Journal of Money, Credit and Banking, 20(3), 559-588.

Glosten, L.R., Jagannathan, R. and Runkie, D. (1989), "Relationship Between the Expected Value and the Volatility of the Nominal Excess Return on Stocks", Banking Research Center Working Paper No.166. Northwestern University, Evanston, IL.

Giovannini, A. (1988), "Exchange Rates and Traded Goods Prices", Journal of International Economics, 24, 45-68.

Goldberg, L.S. (1993), "Exchange Rates and Investment in United States Industry," Review of Economics and Statistics, November; 75(4), 575-588.

Gotur, P. (1985), "Effects of Exchange Rate Volatility on Trade: Some Further Evidence," International Monetary Fund Staff Papers, 32, 475-512.

Grabel, I. (1995a), "Speculation-led economic development: a Post-Keynesian Interpretation of Financial Liberalization Programs in the Third World", International Review of Applied Economics, 9(2), 127-149.

Grabel, I. (1995b), "Assessing the Impact of Financial Liberalisation on Stock Market Volatility in Selected Developing Countries," Journal of Development Studies, 31(6), 903-917.

Gray, Jo Anna, and Magda Kamdil (1991), "Is Price Flexibility Stabilising? A Broader Perspective," Journal of Money, Credit and Banking, February; 23(1), 1-12.

Greenwood, J. (1983), "Expectations, the Exchange Rate and the Current Account", Journal of Monetary Economics, 12, 543-569.

Gultekin, M. and Gultekin, B. (1983), "Stock Market Seasonality: International Evidence", Journal of Financial Economics, 12, 469-482.

Hakkio, C.S. and Morris, C.S., (1984), "Vector Autoregressions: A User's Guide," Discussion Paper No. RWP84-10, Federal Reserve Bank of Kansas City.

Hamilton, J.D. (1994). "Time Series Analysis", Princeton University Press, Princeton, New Jersey.

Harris, M. (1993), "Differences of Opinion make a Horse Race", Review of Financial Studies, 6(3), 473-506.

Hardouvelis, G. (1990), "Margin requirements, volatility and the transitory component of stock prices," American Economic Review, 80, 736-763.

Haugen, R.A. and Jorian, P. (1996), "The January Effect: Still there after all these Years", Financial Analysts Journal, January-February, 27-31.

Hayashi, F. (1982), "Tobin's Marginal q and Average q: A Neoclassical Interpretation", Econometrica, 50, 3-30.

Henderson, D.W. (1979), "Financial Policies in Open Economies," American Economic Review, Papers and Proceedings, 69, 181-202.

Hendry, D.F. (1974), "Stochastic Specification in an Aggregate Demand Model of the United Kingdom," Econometrica, 42, 559-578.

Hendry, D.F. (1977), "On the Time Series Approach to Econometric Model Building," in C.A. Sims (ed.) New Methods in Business Cycle Research, Federal Reserve Bank of Minneapolis.

Hendry, D.F. and Mizon, G.E. (1977), "Serial Correlation as a Convenient Simplification Not a Nuisance: A Comment on a Study of the Demand for Money by the Bank of England," Economic Journal, 88, 549-563.

Heston, S.L. and Rouwehorst, K.G. (1994), "Does Industrial Structure Explain the Benefits of International Diversification," Journal of Financial Economics, August; 36(1), 3-27.

Hicks, J. (1967), Critical Essays in Monetary Theory. Oxford University Press: Oxford.

Higgins, M.L. and Bera, A.K. (1992), "A class of nonlinear ARCH models," International Economic Review, 33, 137-158.

Hjarvey, A. and E. Ruiz, (1994), "Nultivariate Stochastic Variance Models," Review of Economic Studies, April; 61(2), 247-264.

Hooper, P. and Kohlhagen, S.W. (1978), "The Effect of Exchange Rate Uncertainty on the Prices and Volume of International Trade," Journal of International Economics, 8, 483-511.

Hornstein, A. (1993), "Monopolistic Competition, Increasing Returns To Scale, and the Importance of Productivity Shocks," Journal of Monetary Economics, June; 31(3), 299-316.

Hsieh, D.A. (1993), "Chaos and Order in the Capital Markets - A New View of Cycles, Prices and Market Volatility," Journal of Finance, Dec; 48(5), 2041-2044.

Humpage, O.S. and Osterbert, W.P. (1990), "Intervention and foreign exchange risk premium: An empirical investigation of daily effects. Unpublished manuscript (Federal Reserve Bank of Cleveland, Cleveland, OH).

International Monetary Fund, (1984), "Exchange Rate Volatility and World Trade," Occasional Paper No. 28, July.

Jones. C.M. G.Kaul and. Lipson, M.L. (1994) "Information, Trading, and Volatility," Journal of Financial Economics, August; 36(1), 127-154.

Karpoff, J.M. (1987), "The Relation Between Price Changes and Trading Volume," Journal of Financial and Quantitative Analysis, March, 22, 109-126.

Kawai, M. (1985), "Exchange Rates, the Current Account and Monetary-Fiscal Policies in the Short Run and in the Long Run", Oxford Economic Papers, 37, 391-425.

Kearney, C. (1996), "Volatility and Risk in Integrated Financial Systems: Measurement, Transmission and Policy Implications," in F. Bruni, D. Fair and R. O'Brien (eds.), Managing Risk in Volatile Financial Markets, Kluwer Academic Press, Ch 6.

Kearney, C. and Monadjemi, M. (1990), "Fiscal Policy and Current Account Performance: International Evidence on the Twin Deficits," Journal of Macroeconomics, 12-2, 197-219.

Kearney, C. (1990), "Stabilization Policy with Flexible Exchange Rates," in D.T. Llewelling and C.R. Milner (ed), Current Issues in International Monetary Economics, MacMillan Press, Ch.5.

Kearns, P. and Pagan, A. (1993), "Australian Stock Market Volatility: 1875-1987," Economic Record, 69, 205, 163-178.

Kenen, P.B. and Rodrik, D. (1986), "Measuring and Analysing the Effects of Short-term Volatility in Real Exchange Rates," Review of Economics and Statistics, 311-315.

Keynes, J.M. (1963), "On The Theory of a Monetary Economy," in Festschrift fur Arthur Spiethoff (Munich: Duncher & Humblot, 1933); reprinted in Nebraska Journal of Economics and Business, Vol. 2, No.2 Autumn 1963.

Keynes, J.M. (1964), The General Theory of Employment, Interest and Money, New York: Harcourt Brace Jovanovich.

Kim, K.M and Wu, C. (1987), "Macro-economic Factors and Stock Returns," The Journal of Financial Research, 10, 87-98.

King, M. (1994), "Volatility and Links Between National Stock Markets," Econometrica, July; 62(4), 901-933.

King, Stephen, R. (1988), "Is Increased Price Flexibility Stabilising: Comment," American Economic Review, 78, March, 267-272.

Kindleberger, C.P. (1978), "Manias, Panics and Crashes: A History of Financial Crises," New York:Basic Books.

Klein, M.W. (1990), "Sectoral Effects of Exchange Rate Volatility on United States Exports," Journal of International Money and Finance, 9, 299-308.

Kleidon, A.W. (1986), "Variance Bounds Tests and Stock Price Valuation Models," Journal of Political Economy, 95, 953-1001.

Koch, P.D. and Koch, T.W. (1991), "Evolution in Dynamic Linkages across DailyNational Stock Indices," Journal of International Money and Finance, 10, 231-251.

Koray, Faik and Lastrapes, William D. (1989), "Real Exchange Rate Volatility and U.S. Bilateral Trade: A VAR Approach," Review of Economics and Statistics, 71, 708-12.

Koutmos, G., Lee, U. and Theodossiou, P. (1994), "Time-Varying Betas and Volatility Persistence in International Stock Markets," Journal of Economics and Business, 46, 101-112.

Koutoulas, G. and Kryzanowski, L. (1996), "Macrofactor Conditional Volatilities, Time-Varying Risk Premia and Stock Return Behaviour," The Financial

Kramer, C. (1994), "Macroeconomic Seasonality and the January Effect," The Journal of Finance, 49; 5, 1883-1891.

Kroner, F.K. and Lastrapes, W.D. (1993) "The impact of exchange rate volatility on international trade: reduced form estimates using the GARCH-in-mean model," Journal of International Money and Finance, 12, 298-318.

Kupiec, P.H. (1991), "Stock Market Volatility in OECD Countries: Recent Trends, Consequences for the Real Economy, And Proposals for Reform," Economic Studies, No.17, Autumn.

Kupiec, P.H. (1993), "Do Stock Prices Exhibit Excess Volatility. Frequently Deviate from Fundamental Values and Generally Behave Inefficiently?," Financial Markets, Institutions and Instruments, January, 2. 1-61.

Kumar, R. and Dhawan, R. (1991), "Exchange Rate Volatility and Pakistan's Exports to the Developed World, 1974-85," World Development, 19(9), 1225-40.

Kyland, F.E. and Prescott, E.F. (1982), "Testing Structural Hypothesis in a Multivariate Cointegration Analysis of the PPP and the UIP for UK," Journal of Econometrics, 47, 1345-70.

Lamoureux , C.G. and Lastrapes, W.D. (1990), "Heteroskedasticity in stock return data volume versus GARCH effects," The Journal of Finance, 45, 221-229.

Latané, H. and Riddleman, R. (1976), " Standard Deviations of Stock Price Ratios Implied in Option Prices," Journal of Finance, 31 May 1976, 369-81.

Lee, T.K. (1988), "Does conditional covariance or conditional variance explain time varying risk premia in foreign exchange returns?" Economic Letters, 27, 371-373.

LeRoy, Stephen F. and Porter, Richard D. (1981), "The Present Value Relation Tests Based on Implied Variance Bounds," Econometrica, May; 49(3), 555-574.

LeRoy, Stephen F. and Parke, William R. (1992), "Stock Price Volatility: Tests Based on the Geometric Random Walk," American Economic Review, September, 82(4), 981-992.

Lucas, R.E. Jnr (1976), "Econometric Policy Evaluation: A Critique" in K. Brunner and A.H. Meltzer (eds.), The Phillips Curve and Labour Markets, North Holland.

Ljung, G.M. and Box, G.E.P. (1978), "On a measure of lag of fit in time series models," Biometrika, 67, 297-303.

Magee, S.P. (1974), "U.S. import prices in the currency contract period," Brookings Papers on Economic Activity, 1, 117-164.

Makin, J.H. (1976), "Eurocurrencies and the Evolution of the International Monetary System", Eurocurrencies and the International Monetary System," ed. by Stem, C.H., Makin, J.H. and Logue, D.E., American Enterprise Institute for Public Policy Research, 17-52. Spring 87.

Malliaris, A.G. and Urrutia, J.L. (1992), "The International Crash of October 1987: Causality Tests", Journal of Financial and Quantitative Analysis, 27; 3, 353-364.

Malkiel, B. (1979), "The capital formation problem in the United States," Journal of Finance, 34, 291-306.

Mandelbrot, B. (1963), "The variation of certain speculative prices," Journal of Business, 36, 394-419.

Marston, R.C. (1985), Stabilization Policies in Open Economies, in R.W. Jones and P.B. Kenen (eds.), Handbook of International Economics, Elsevier Science.

Marsh, T.A. and Merton, R.C. (1986), "Dividend Variability and Variance Bounds for the Rationality of Stock Market Prices," American Economic Review, 73, 483-498.

Mascaro, Angelo and Meltzer, Allan H. (1983), "Long- and Short-Term Interest Rates in a Risky World," Journal of Monetary Economics, November, 12, 485-518.

McAleer, M. and McKenzie, C.R. (1991), "When are Two Step Estimators Efficient?", Econometric Reviews, 10, 235-252.

McMillin, W. Douglas. (1988), "Money Growth Volatility and the Macroeconomy," Journal of Money, Credit and Banking, August, 20, 3, 319-335.

Medhora, R. (1990), "The Effect of Exchange Rate Volatility on Trade: The Case of the West African Monetary Union's Imports," World Development, 18(2), 313-24.

Meese, R.A. and Rogoff, K. (1983), "The Out-of-Sample Failure of Empirical Exchange Rate Models: Sampling Error or Misspecification?," in J.A. Frankel (ed), Exchange Rates and International Macroeconomics, pp. 67-105, Chicago: University of Chicago Press, IL.

Merton, R.C. (1980), "On Estimating the Expected Return on the Market: An Exploratory Investigation," Journal of Financial Economics, 8, 323-361.

Merton, Robert C. (1987), "A Simple Model of Capital Market Equilibrium with Incomplete Information," Journal of Finance, July; 42(3), 483-510.

Minsky, H.P. (1972), "Financial Stability Revisited: The Economics of Disaster," Reappraisal of the Discount Mechanism, Vol. 3. Washington: Board of Governors Federal Reserve System.

Minsky, H.P. (1977), "The Financial Instability Hypothesis: An Interpretation of Keynes and an alternative to 'Standard' Theory," Nebraska Journal of Economics and Business, 16, 5-16.

Miller, M.H. and Neuberger, A. (1993), "Financial Innovations and Market Volatility," Economica, Feburary; 60(237), 115-116.

Milbourne, R. (1995), "Money and Monetary Policy," in P. Kriesler (ed), The Australian Economy, Allen and Unwin, 119-141.

Mizon, G. (1995), "Progressive Modelling of Macroeconomic Time Series: The LSE Methodology," in K.D. Hoover (ed), Macroeconometrics; Developments, Tensions and Prospects, Kluwer Academic Publishers, Boston.

Modigliani, F. and Miller, M.H. (1958), "The Cost of Capital, Corporation Finance and the Theory of Investment," American Economic Review, Vol 42, 511-532.

Moore, B. (1988), "Unpacking the Post-Keynesian Black Box: Wages, Bank Lending and Money Supply," in P. Arestis (ed), Post-Keynesian Monetary Economics, Edward Elgar Publishing, 122-151.

Morgan, D. (1990), "Evolution of Monetary Policy since Financial Deregulation," Economic Papers, December Vol.9, No.4, 1-18.

Muller, U.A., R.J. Nagler and Olsen, R.B. (1993), "A Geographical Model for the Daily and Weekly Seasonal Volatility in the Foreign Exchange Market," Journal of International Money and Finance, August; 12(4), 413-438.

Mundaca, B.G. (1990), "Intervention decisions and exchange rate volatility in a target zone," Unpublished manuscript (Research Department, Norges Bank, Oslo)

Mundell, R.A. (1963), "Capital Mobility and Stabilization Policy Under Fixed and Flexible Exchange Rates," Canadian Journal of Economic and Political Science, 29, 475-485.

Mussa, M. (1980), "The Role of the Current Account in Exchange Rate Dynamics," Centre for Mathematical Studies in Business and Economics, Report No. 8033, University of Chicago.

Needham, N. (1986), "The Effect of Exchange Rate Volatility on the Price and Volume of Australian Bilateral Trade," Reserve Bank of Australia, Conference of Economists, Monash University, 1986.

Nelson, D.B. (1990), "Stationarity and Persistence in the GARCH(1,1) Model," Econometric Theory, 6, 318-334.

Nelson, D.B. (1991), "Conditional Heteroskedasticity in Asset Returns: A new approach," Econometrica, 59, 347-370.

Nelson, D.B. and Foster, D.P. (1994), "Asymptotic Filtering Theory for Univariate ARCH Models," Econometrica, 62, 1-41.

Nelson, D.B. (1996), "Modelling Stock Market Volatility Changes," in P. Rossi (ed), Modelling Stock Market Volatility, Academic Press, 3-15.

Ng, V.K. and Pirrong, S.C. (1994), "Fundamentals and Volatility - Storage, Spreads, and the Volatility of Metals Prices," Journal of Finance, 49(3), 1086-1087.

Nicholas, N.A. (1993),"Efficient - Chaotic - What's the New Finance," Harvard Business Review,. March-April; 71(2), 50.

O.Scott, L.O. (1991), "Financial Market Volatility," IMF Staff Papers, 38, No.3, September.

Obstfeld, M. (1981), "Macroeconomic Policy, Exchange Rate Dynamics and Optimal Asset Accumulation," Journal of Political Economy, 89, 1142-1161.

Officer, R.R. (1973), "The Variability of the Market Factor of the New York Stock Exchange," Journal of Business, 46, 434-453.

Oxley, L. and McAleer, M. (1993), "Econometric Issues in Macroeconomic Models with Generated Regressors," Journal of Economic Surveys, 7, 1-40.

Pagan, A. (1984), "Econometric Issues in the Analysis of Regressions with Generated Regressors," International Economic Review, 25, 221-247.

Pagan, A. (1986), "Two Stage and Related Estimators and their Applications," Review of Economic Studies, 53, 517-538.

Pagan, A. and Schwert, G.W. (1989), "Alternative models for conditional stock volatility," Journal of Econometrics, 45, 267-290.

Peel, D.A., Pope, P.F. and Yadav, P.K. (1993), "Deregulation and the Volatility of UK Stock Prices," Journal of Business Finance and Accounting, 20; (3), 359-372.

Pentcost, E.J. (1993), "Exchange Rate Dynamics," Edward Elgar Publishing Limited.

Persson, T. (1984), "Deficits and Intergenerational Welfare in Open Economies," University of Stockholm Institute of International Studies Seminar Paper No.30.

Pesaran, B. and Robinson, G. (1993), "The European Exchange Rate Mechanism and the Volatility of the Sterling Deutschemark Exchange Rate," Economic Journal. November; 103(421), 1418-1431.

Peters. E.E. and Hommes, C. (1993), "Chaos and order in the Capital Markets - A New View of Cycles, Prices and Market Volatility," Economist 141(4), 586-588.

Phillips, P.C. and Perron, P. (1986), "Testing for Unit Roots in Time Series Regressions,"

Phillips, P.C.B (1987), "Time Series Regressions with a Unit Root", Econometrica, 55, 277-301.

Phillips, P.C.B. and Perron, P. (1988), "Testing for a Unit Root in Time Series Regressions," Biometrika, 65, 335-346.

Pindyck, R. (1984), "Risk, Inflation and Stock Markets," American Economic Review, 74, 335-351.

Plosser, C.I. (1982), "Government Financing Decisions and Asset Returns," Journal of Monetary Economics, 9, 325-352.

Poterba, J.M and Summers, L.H. (1986), "The Persistence of Volatility and Stock Market Fluctuations," American Economic Review, 76, 1142-1151.

Rahman, H. and Yung, K. (1994), "Atlantic and Pacific Stock Markets - Correlation and Volatility Transmission", Global Finance Journal, 5, 103-119.

Ratner, M. (1993), "A Cointegration Test of the Impact of Foreign Exchange Rates on US Stock Market Prices," Global Finance Journal, 4, 93-101.

Robson, G.B and Gallagher, C.C (1994), "Change in the Size Distribution of U.K. Firms," Small Business Economics. August: 6(4): 299-312.

Rodriguez, C.A. (1979), "Short and Long Run Effects of Monetary and Fiscal Policies Under Flexible Exchange Rates and Perfect Capital Mobility," American Economic Review, 69, 176-182

Rogers, J.H. (1994), "Entry Barriers and Price Movements Between Major and Emerging Stock," Journal of Macroeconomics. Spring; 16(2), 221-241.

Romer, Christina D. (1986), "Spurious Volatility in Historical Unemployment Data," Journal of Political Economy, 94, February, 1-37.

Romer, Christina D. (1989), "The Pre-War Business Cycle Reconsidered: New Estimates of Gross National Product, 1869-1908," Journal of Political Economy, 97, February, 1-37.

Rothschild, M. and Stiglitz, J.E. (1971), "Increasing risk II: Its economic consequences," Journal of Economic Theory, 3, 66-84.

Sachs, J.D. (1983), "Aspects of the Current Account Behaviour of OECD Economies," in E. Claassen and P. Salin (eds.), Recent Issues in the Theory of Flexible Exchange Rates, (North Holland), 101-128.

Samuels, J.M. and Yacout, N. (1981), "Stock Exchanges in Developing Countries," Savings and Development, Vol. V, No. 4, pp. 217-30.

Schwartz, G. W. (1978), "Estimating the Dimension of a Model," Annals of Statistics, 6, 461-464.

Schwert, G.W. (1988), "Business Cycles, Financial Crises and Stock Volatility," Mimeo. University of Rochester, William E. Simon Graduate School of Business, Rochester, NY.

Schwert, G.W. (1989), "Why Does Stock Market Volatility Change Over Time?," Journal of Finance, 54:5, 1115-1151.

Schwert, G.W. (1990), "Stock Market Volatility," Financial Analyst Journal, May-June, Vol 46, 23-34.

Schwert, G.W. (1991), "Review of Market Volatility by Robert J. Shiller," Journal of Portfolio Management, Summer, 17, 74-78.

Scott, L.O. (1991), "Financial Market Volatility: A Survey," International Monetary Fund Staff Papers, 38; 3, 582-625.

Shiller, Robert J. (1981), "Do Stock Prices Move Too Much to be Justified by Subsequent Changes in Dividends?," American Economic Review, June, 71,3, 421-436.

Shiller, Robert J. (1984), "Stock Prices and Social Dynamics," Brookings Papers on Economic Activity, 2, 457-498.

Shiller, Robert J. (1989), Market Volatility. The MIT Press, Cambridge, Massachusetts (USA).

Sims, C. (1980), "Macroeconomics and Reality," Econometrica, 48, 1-48.

Singh, A. (1993), "Should Developing Countries Encourage Stock Markets?" United Nations Conference on Trade and Development Review, 11-22.

Smaghi, Lorenzo Bini, 1990, "Exchange Rate Variability and Trade: Why is it so Difficult to Find Any Empirical Relationship?," Banca d'Italia, Discussion Paper.

Snowden, P. (1987), "Financial market liberalisation in LDCs," Journal of Development Studies, 24(1), 83-93.

Spiro, S.P. (1990), "Book Review: Market Volatility," Financial Analyst Journal, September-October, 24, 80.

Subrahmanyam, A. (1994), "Circuit Breakers and Market Volatility - A Theoretical Perspective," Journal of Finance, March, 49(1), 237-254.

Sundararajan, B. and Balino, T. (Eds.) (1991), Banking Crises: Cases and Issues, Washington, DC: IMF.

Szpiro, G.G. (1994), "Exchange Rate Speculation and Chaos Inducing Intervention," Journal of Economic Behaviour and Organisation. Aug; 24(3), 363-368

Tarhan, V. (1993), "Policy and Volatility of Asset Returns," Journal of Economics and Business. August; 45(3-4), 269-283.

Tatom, J.A. (1984), "Interest Rate Variability: Its Links to the Variability of Monetary Growth and Economic Performance," Economic Review, The Federal Reserve Bank of St. Louis, November 66, 31-47.

Tatom, John A. (1985), "Interest Rate Variability and Economic Performance: Further Evidence," Journal of Political Economy, October, 93, 1008-1018.

Taylor, John B. (1986), "Improvements in Macroeconomic Stability: The Role of Wages and Prices," in Robert J. Gordon (ed.), The American Business Cycle: Continuity and Change, 639-677, University of Chicago Press.

Tobin,J. (1958), "Liquidity Preference as Behavior Towards Risk," Review of Economic Studies, 25, February, 65-86.

Tobin, J. (1969), "A General Equilibrium Approach to Monetary Theory," Journal Money Credit and Banking, 1, 15-29.

Timmermann, A.G. (1993), "How Learning in Financial Markets generates Excess Volatility and Predictability in Stock Prices," Quarterly Journal of Economics, 108, 4, 1135-5533.

Vannorden, S. and Schaller, H. (1993), "The Predictability of Stock Market Regime - Evidence from the Toronto Stock Exchange," Review of Economics and Statistics. August; 75(3), 505-510.

Viaene, Jean-Marie, (1992). "International trade and exchange rate volatility," European EconomicReview, 36, 1311-1321.

Wang, G.H.K. and Mickalski, R.J. (1994), "An Intraday Analysis of Bid - Ask Spreads and Price Volatility in the Standard and Poor 500 Index Futures Market," Journal of Futures Markets, Oct: 14(7), 837-859.

West, Kenneth D. (1988), "Bubbles, Fads and Stock Price Volatility Tests: A Partial View," Journal of Finance, July, 43(3), 639-656.

Willett, T.D. "Exchange Rate Volatility, International Trade and Resource Allocation: A Perspective on Recent Research," Journal of International Money and Finance, Supplement, March 5, S101-S112.

Williams, J.B. (1938), "The Theory of Investment Value," Cambridge Massachusetts: Harvard University Press.

Wolfson, M.H. (1986), "Financial Crises," Armonk: M.E. Sharpe.

Wolfson, M.H. (1990), "The causes of financial instability," Journal of Post-Keynesian Economics, 12(3), 333-55.

Zellner, A. (1979), "Causality and Econometrics," in K. Brunner and A. Meltzer (eds.), Three Aspects of Policy and Policymaking: Knowledge, Data and Institutions, Carnegie-Rochester Conference Series on Public Policy No.10, (North Holland), 9-54.

Zellner, A. and Palm, F., (1974), "Time Series Analysis and Simultaneous Equation Econometric Models," Journal of Econometrics, 8, 17-54.